Indo-U.S. Civil Nuclear Deal

Indo-U.S. Civil Nuclear Deal

Volume–2

Edited by

Rahul Bhonsle
Ved Prakash
K.R. Gupta

ATLANTIC

PUBLISHERS & DISTRIBUTORS (P) LTD

Published by

ATLANTIC

PUBLISHERS & DISTRIBUTORS (P) LTD

B-2, Vishal Enclave, Opp. Rajouri Garden,
New Delhi-110027
Phones : 25413460, 25429987, 25466842

Sales Office
7/22, Ansari Road, Darya Ganj,
New Delhi–110002
Phones : 23273880, 23275880, 23280451
Fax : 91-11-23285873
web : www.atlanticbooks.com
e-mail : info@atlanticbooks.com

ISBN 81-269-0713-4 Vol. 1
ISBN 81-269-0714-2 Vol. 2
ISBN 81-269-0715-0 Set

Printed in India
at Nice Printing Press, Delhi

Preface

The Indo-U.S. Civil Nuclear Deal is seen as the most significant development giving implicit formal recognition to India's nuclear weapons status and a possible opening up of opportunities for it to become a global player in the field of nuclear energy. The wording in the July 18, 2005 joint statement between India and the U.S. provides an essence of the deal: India with its strong commitment to preventing WMD proliferation and as a responsible state with advanced nuclear technology, should acquire the same benefits and advantages, reciprocally assuming the same responsibilities and practices as other leading nations with advanced nuclear technology, such as the P-5.

Apart from non-proliferation, the U.S. President and the Indian Prime Minister have agreed on a large number of initiatives for economic prosperity, energy security, clean environment, knowledge partnership, global safety and security, deepening democracy and meeting international challenges. President Bush has called India in the 21st century as a natural partner of the United States. The successful transformation of the U.S.-India relationship is said to have a decisive and positive influence on the future international system as it evolves in this New Century.

The Indo-U.S. Civil Nuclear Deal is an attempt to create a delicate balance between the policies pursued by India, the Nuclear Suppliers Group as well as the nuclear non-proliferation watchdog, the International Atomic Energy Agency. It is a recognition of the fact that in a world facing severe energy crisis with escalating oil prices and rampant environmental pollution due to consumption of conventional sources of energy, it is illogical to deny clean fuel to India, which though a non-signatory to the Non-proliferation Treaty, has not violated any legal commitment and never encouraged proliferation of nuclear weapons.

Some experts view this deal as the United States' attempt to create a new global balance of power in order to counter the rising power of China. Others feel that the Deal is a discrimination in favor of India which would set an indefensible precedent as the U.S. struggles to curb the nuclear programs of countries like Iran and North Korea. Back home, there are many apprehensions that India will have to surrender some of its sovereign rights in order to receive new nuclear reactor units from abroad and fuel for new or existing reactors from the members of NPT. Some critics say the U.S. would not provide India with the state-of-the-art enrichment technology and equipment since its domestic law prohibits such a trade. On the other side, we have scientists, including no less a person than the former chairman of India's AEC, asserting publicly that India is so far ahead of the world in the fields of fast breeder reactors and nuclear reactor safety that they will come to us seeking help. Experts advocating the Indo-U.S. Civil Nuclear Deal hold that India should learn from China — perhaps their model of economic development. It is scouring all over the world, for energy to ensure its economic development. Look at the way it subjected itself to additional political conditionalities that Australia insisted upon for supplying uranium which China as an NPT-signatory could have resisted. That is pragmatism, demanded by long-term national interest. And what are the Indian 'patriots' doing? Fulminating at the trivialities: U.S.A. is changing goalposts, even when the final 123 Agreement is yet months away. In the same vein, they talk of India losing its autonomy in the nuclear decision-making on far-fetched reasoning. With such kind of facetious arguments, they may end up tying executive's hands, leaving it no space or flexibility to clinch the agreement in the final stages. Any bilateral agreement, by its very definition, is a function of give and take. If the U.S. has executed a near-u-turn in its non-proliferation policy to befriend India, the latter too must make some concessions somewhere, of course, without affecting its strategic interests. In international affairs, nothing comes free. Only beggars accept charity!

Chinese pragmatism deserves high praise. It has an over $200 billion annual trade deficit with the U.S., has invested $250 billion in the U.S. bonds and banks, and is a partner with U.S. in a number of international economic and technological arrangements. The critics of the Indo-U.S. Civil Nuclear Deal should expend their energy in convincing Indians to follow and emulate the Chinese pragmatism than on rustling up inane and venal arguments to oppose the Deal.

Indians must realise that power, economic and military, and especially the latter, is the currency of the international community. If India had not done what it did in 1998, the U.S.A. would not have offered it the strategic partnership. Weakness invites scorn, and at times, even aggression, even by a small neighbour. To wit, Pakistan attacked India in September 1965 because it was perceived to be 'weak' at that point of time. Indians must resolve that their country would never be perceived weak by any one or any nation in future.

As the Deal has to be approved not only by the legislative leg of the Washington power tripod but it must also clear hurdles in forty-five capitals in Europe, Asia and the Americas, which are tightly knit under the rubric of the Nuclear Suppliers Group (NSG), the action is not thus restricted within the U.S.

and India but spread worldwide and accordingly the reactions on the Deal are mixed.

The issue of the Indo-U.S. Civil Nuclear Deal is thus extremely complex involving national and international polity, nuclear non-proliferation, diplomacy as well as technicalities of the nuclear fuel cycle. This is also an important test case for both the United States as well as India to place their relationship in a new paradigm of collaborated acceleration rather than inconsistent progress in fits and starts. In the process, we will also be testing new waters of acceptance of India as a nuclear weapons state by the international community in general and the nations in our immediate neighborhood, China and Pakistan in particular. The present book in two Volumes thus attempts to provide a holistic perspective of the Indo-U.S. Civil Nuclear Deal in the context of international relations, economic as well as nuclear energy cooperation.

The book includes articles contributed by erudite experts in the field of international strategic affairs. It also consolidates in one source important documents relating to the Civil Nuclear Deal, e.g. speeches of the U.S. President, George W Bush, Indian Prime Minister, Mr Manmohan Singh, Senators, Congressmen, senior officials like Ms Condoleezza Rice, Nicholas Burns, Shyam Saran, the viewpoints of different countries, the Nuclear Suppliers Group and International Atomic Energy Agency Chief, ElBaradei. When different experts contribute papers on the same subject, some duplication becomes unavoidable. The Editors have not attempted to remove duplication with a view to provide the entire context in which the papers have been written by the authors.

The book is thus a Pone source primer on the Indo-U.S. Civil Nuclear Deal and will be found useful by students of strategic affairs and international relations. It will be helpful for Government executives, strategic analysts and parliamentarians, both of India and the United States. Common readers interested in current world affairs, Indo-U.S. relations and nuclear issues would also find the book interesting and useful.

Rahul Bhonsle
Ved Prakash
K.R. Gupta

Contents

Pages

VOLUME–2

Excerpts from PM's Reply to Discussion in Rajya Sabha on Civil Nuclear Energy Cooperation with the United States

8

August 17, 2006

1. At the outset, I would like to convey my gratitude to all the Hon'ble Members who have participated in this debate. I am grateful for this opportunity to clarify some of the issues arising from the discussion. I will do so in a non-partisan spirit and I have every reason to believe that after I have finished that I will be able to carry the whole House with me. Our Government has never shied away from a full discussion in Parliament on this important issue. On three previous occasions on July 29, 2005, February 27, 2006 and March 7, 2006, I had made detailed statements and discussed this important subject in this august House. Once again, several issues have been raised during the current discussions and I wish to take this opportunity to respond to them. I also intend to cover developments since my last Suo Moto statement of March 7 this year.

2. Two types of comments have been made during the discussion in the House. The first set of issues pertains to the basic orientation of our foreign policy. Some Hon'ble Members have observed that by engaging in discussions with, and allegedly acquiescing in the demands made by the United States, we have compromised the independent nature of our foreign policy.

3. The second set of issues pertain to deviations from the July 18 Joint Statement and the March 2 Separation Plan. Many of the points raised by the Hon'ble Members have also been aired outside Parliament, notably also by some senior members of the scientific establishment. Overall, a listing of the important concerns include the following: that the India-U.S. Nuclear initiative and more particularly the content of the proposed legislation in the U.S. Congress, could undermine the autonomy

of our decision-making; limit the options or compromise the integrity of our strategic program; and adversely affect the future of our scientific research and development. To sum up, this would suggest that India's strategic nuclear autonomy is being compromised and India is allowing itself to be pressurized into accepting new and unacceptable conditions that are deviations from the commitments made by me to Parliament in July 2005 and in February and March this year.

4. I recognize that many of these concerns are borne out of genuine conviction that nothing should be done that would undermine long standing policies that have a bearing on India's vital national security interests. I fully share and subscribe to these sentiments. I would like to assure the Hon'ble Members that negotiations with the U.S. regarding the civilian nuclear deal have not led to any change in the basic orientation of our policies, or affected our independent judgment of issues of national interest. Last year, during my visit to the U.S., I addressed the National Press Club in the full glare of the media. A question was put to me regarding what I thought about the U.S. intervention in Iraq. In the full public glare of the media I said that it was a mistake. I said the same to President Bush when he visited India. I said India does not find favor with regime change.

5. The thrust of our foreign policy remains the promotion of our national interest. We are unswerving in our commitment to an independent foreign policy. We do recognize the complexities present in an increasingly inter-dependent and multi-polar world. While we recognize that the United States is a pre-eminent power and good relations with the U.S. are in our national interest, this has not in any way clouded our judgment. There are many areas of agreement with the United States, but at the same time there are a number of areas in which we have differences and we have not shied away from making these known to the U.S., as also expressing them in public. Currently, we are engaged not only with the U.S. but other global powers like Russia, China, the EU, U.K., France and Japan. We are also focusing on ASEAN, as well as countries in West Asia, Africa

and Latin America. More importantly, we are devoting proportionately larger time and effort in building relations with countries in our immediate neighbourhood like Nepal, Bhutan, Sri Lanka, Bangladesh, Myanmar, and Pakistan. Our relations with all these countries are determined by the dictates of our enlightened national interest and we have not allowed any other country, including the United States, to influence our polices. This will not change as long as I am Prime Minister.

6. I would, hence, again reiterate in view of the apprehensions expressed, that the proposed U.S. legislation on nuclear cooperation with India will not be allowed to become an instrument to compromise India's sovereignty. Our foreign policy is determined solely by our national interests. No legislation enacted in a foreign country can take away from us that sovereign right. Thus, there is no question of India being bound by a law passed by a foreign legislature. Our sole guiding principle in regard to our foreign policy, whether it is on Iran or any other country, will be dictated entirely by our national interest.

7. Let me now turn to some of the concerns that have been expressed on the second set of issues regarding possible deviations from assurances given by me in this august House on the July 18, 2005 Joint Statement and the March 2, 2006 Separation Plan. I would like to state categorically that there have neither been nor will there be any compromises on this score and the Government will not allow such compromises to occur in the future.

8. Hon'ble Members will recall that during President Bush's visit to India in March this year, agreement was reached between India and the United States on a Separation Plan in implementation of the India-United States Joint Statement of July 18, 2005. This Separation Plan had identified the nuclear facilities that India was willing to offer, in a phased manner, for IAEA safeguards, contingent on reciprocal actions taken by the United States. For its part, the United States Administration was required to approach the U.S. Congress for amending its laws and the Nuclear Suppliers Group for adapting its guidelines to

enable full civilian nuclear cooperation between India and the international community.

9. The U.S. administration had thereafter approached the U.S. Congress to amend certain provisions of the United States Atomic Energy Act of 1954, which currently prohibit civil nuclear cooperation with India. The U.S. House of Representatives International Relations Committee passed a Bill on the subject on 27th June 2006. The House of Representatives passed the Bill as approved by its International Relations Committee on July 27.

10. The Senate Foreign Relations Committee passed its version of the Bill on June 29, 2006. The U.S. Senate is now expected to vote on this version of the Bill some time in September. We have concerns over both the House and Senate versions of the Bill. Since the two Bills are somewhat different in content, according to U.S. practice they will need to be reconciled to produce a single piece of legislation. After adoption by both the House and the Senate, this would become law when the U.S. President accords his approval. The final shape of the legislation would, therefore, be apparent only when the House and the Senate complete the second stage of assent/adoption.

11. Meanwhile, the U.S. Government has approached the Nuclear Suppliers Group to adapt its guidelines to enable full civil nuclear cooperation between India and the International community. In March this year, the NSG at its plenary meeting in Brazil held a preliminary discussion on this issue. The matter will be further discussed by the Nuclear Suppliers Group later this year. On our part, we have separately raised this issue with several countries and urged them to lift the existing restrictions on nuclear supplies to India. I myself have raised this issue with the Heads of State or Government of Russia, France, U.K., Japan, Germany, Brazil, Norway, Iceland and Cyprus, among others.

12. In view of the concerns voiced by the Hon'ble Members, I shall try to address each of these concerns in some detail. I shall, however, begin by affirming that our approach is guided by the understandings contained in the July 2005 Joint Statement

and the March 2006 Separation Plan. What we can agree with the United States to enable nuclear cooperation must be strictly within these parameters.

13. The key provisions to which references have been made in Parliament and outside are the following:

(i) *Full Civil Nuclear Cooperation* : The central imperative in our discussions with the United States on Civil Nuclear Cooperation is to ensure the complete and irreversible removal of existing restrictions imposed on India through iniquitous restrictive trading regimes over the years. We seek the removal of restrictions on all aspects of cooperation and technology transfers pertaining to civil nuclear energy—ranging from nuclear fuel, nuclear reactors, to re-processing spent fuel, i.e. all aspects of a complete nuclear fuel cycle.

This will be the surest guarantee of India's acceptance as a full and equal partner of the international nuclear community, even while preserving the integrity of our three stage nuclear program and protecting the autonomy of our scientific research and development. We will not agree to any dilution that would prevent us from securing the benefits of full civil nuclear cooperation as amplified above.

(ii) *Principle of Reciprocity*: I had earlier assured the House that reciprocity is the key to the implementation of our understanding contained in the July 2005 Statement. I stand by that commitment. When we put forward the Separation Plan, we again made it clear to the United States that India could not be expected to take on obligations such as placing its nuclear facilities under safeguards in anticipation of future lifting of restrictions. India and the United States have held one round of discussions on a proposed bilateral cooperation agreement. India and the IAEA have held technical discussions regarding an India-Specific Safeguards Agreement. Further discussions are required on both these documents. While these parallel efforts are underway, our position is that we will accept only IAEA safeguards on the nuclear facilities, in a phased manner, and as identified for that purpose in the Separation Plan only when all nuclear restrictions on India have been lifted. On July 29 last year, I had stated that before voluntarily placing our civil nuclear facilities under IAEA safeguards, we will ensure that all restrictions on India have been lifted. There has been no shift in our position on this point.

(iii) *Certification*: The draft Senate Bill requires the U.S. President to make an annual report to the Congress that includes certification that India is in full compliance of its non-proliferation and other commitments. We have made it clear to the United States our opposition to these provisions, even if they are projected as non-binding on India, as being contrary to the letter and spirit of the July Statement. We have told the U.S. administration that the effect of such certification will be to diminish a permanent waiver authority into an annual one. We have also indicated that this would introduce an element of uncertainty regarding future cooperation and is, not acceptable to us.

(iv) *India as a State Possessing Advanced Nuclear Technology*: Hon'ble Members may recall that the July Statement, had acknowledged that India should be regarded as a State with advanced nuclear technology enjoying the same advantages and benefits as other states with advanced nuclear technology, such as the U.S. The July Statement did not refer to India as a Nuclear Weapons State because that has a particular connotation in the NPT but it explicitly acknowledged the existence of India's military nuclear facilities. It also meant that India would not attract full-scope safeguards such as those applied to Non-Nuclear Weapon States that are signatories to the NPT and there would be no curbs on continuation of India's nuclear weapon related activities. In these important respects, India would be very much on par with the five Nuclear Weapon States who are signatories to the NPT. Similarly, the Separation Plan provided for an India-specific safeguards agreement with the IAEA with assurances of uninterrupted supply of fuel to reactors together with India's right to take corrective measures in the event fuel supplies are interrupted. We have made clear to the U.S. that India's strategic programme is totally outside the purview of the July Statement, and we oppose any legislative provisions that mandate scrutiny of either our nuclear weapons program or our unsafeguarded nuclear facilities.

(v) *Safeguards Agreement and Fuel Assurances*: In this respect too, it is worth emphasizing that the March 2006 Separation Plan provides for an India-Specific Safeguards Agreement with the IAEA, with assurances of uninterrupted supply of fuel to reactors that would be placed under IAEA safeguards together with India's right to take corrective measures in the event fuel supplies are interrupted. We, of course, have the sovereign right to take all appropriate measures to fully safeguard our interests. An important assurance is the commitment of support for India's right to build up strategic reserves of nuclear fuel over the lifetime of India's reactors. We have initiated technical discussions at the expert level with the IAEA on an India-Specific Safeguards Agreement. Both the Bilateral Nuclear Cooperation Agreement with the United States and the India-Specific Safeguards Agreement with the IAEA would be only within the parameters of the July Statement and the March Separation Plan. There is no question of India signing either a Safeguards Agreement with the IAEA or an Additional Protocol of a type concluded by Non-Nuclear Weapons States who have signed the NPT. We will not accept any verification measures regarding our safeguarded nuclear facilities beyond those contained in an India-Specific Safeguards Agreement with the IAEA. Therefore there is no question of allowing American inspectors to roam around our nuclear facilities.

(vi) *Integrity and Reliability of Our Strategic Program—Autonomy of Decision-making and Future Scientific Research and Development*: In my statement of March 7, 2006, I had assured Parliament that the Separation Plan would not adversely affect our strategic program. I reiterate that commitment today. The Separation Plan has been so designed as to ensure adequacy of fissile material and other inputs for our strategic program, based on our current and assessed future needs. The integrity of our 3-Stage nuclear program will not be affected. The autonomy of our Research and Development activity, including development of our fast breeder reactors and the thorium program, in the nuclear field will remain unaffected. We will not accept interference by other countries vis-à-vis the development of our strategic program. We will not allow external scrutiny of our strategic program in any manner, much less allow it to be a condition for future nuclear cooperation between India and the international community.

(vii) *Moratorium on Production of Fissile Material*: Our position on this matter is unambiguous. We are not willing to accept a moratorium on the production of fissile material. We are only committed to negotiate a Fissile Material Cut-off Treaty in the Conference on Disarmament in Geneva, a commitment which was given by the previous government. India is willing to join only a non-discriminatory, multilaterally negotiated and internationally verifiable FMCT, as and when it is concluded in the Conference on Disarmament, again provided our security interests are fully addressed.

(viii) *Non-discriminatory Global Nuclear Disarmament*: Our commitment towards non-discriminatory global nuclear disarmament remains unwavering, in line with the Rajiv Gandhi Action Plan. There is no dilution on this count. We do not accept proposals put forward from time to time for regional non-proliferation or regional disarmament. Pending global nuclear disarmament, there is no question of India joining the NPT as a non-nuclear weapons state, or accepting full-scope safeguards as a requirement for nuclear supplies to India, now or in the future.

(ix) *Cessation of Future Cooperation*: There is provision in the proposed U.S. law that were India to detonate a nuclear explosive device, the U.S. will have the right to cease further cooperation. Our position on this is unambiguous. The U.S. has been intimated that reference to nuclear detonation in the India-U.S. Bilateral Nuclear Cooperation Agreement as a condition for future cooperation is not acceptable to us. We are not prepared to go beyond a unilateral voluntary moratorium on nuclear testing as indicated in the July Statement. The same is true of other intrusive non-proliferation benchmarks that are mentioned in the proposed U.S. legislation. India's possession and development of nuclear weapons is an integral part of our national security. This will remain so.

14. Hon'ble Members will appreciate the fact that an international negotiation on nuclear energy cooperation particularly when it involves dismantling restrictive regimes that have lasted for over three decades is a complex and sensitive exercise. What we are attempting today is to put in place new international arrangements that would overturn three decades of iniquitous restrictions. It is inevitable, therefore, that there would be some contradictory pulls and pressures. This does not mean that India will succumb to pressures or accept conditionalities that are contrary to its national interests.

15. I had personally spoken to President Bush in St. Petersburg last month on this issue, and conveyed to him that the proposed U.S. legislation must conform strictly to the parameters of the July 18, 2005 Statement and the March 2, 2006 Separation Plan. This alone would be an acceptable basis

for nuclear cooperation between India and the United States. India cannot, and is not prepared to take on additional commitments outside this agreed framework or allow any extraneous issues to be introduced. I have received an assurance from the U.S. President that it was not his intention to shift goalposts, and that the parameters of the scope of cooperation would be those contained in the July 2005 Joint Statement and the March 2006 Separation Plan. A White House Statement of Administration Policy of July 26, 2006 recognizes some, though not all, of India's concerns, and conveyed that the Administration has voiced them with the Congress.

16. I can assure you that there is no ambiguity in our position in so far as it has been conveyed to the U.S. The U.S. is aware of our position that the only way forward is strict adherence to July Statement and March Separation Plan. I am hopeful that the bilateral India-U.S. Civil Nuclear Cooperation Agreement when concluded will take into account the issues raised here. However, I must be honest and frank that I cannot predict with certainty the final form of the U.S. legislation or the outcome of this process with the NSG, which consists of 45 countries with divergent views. We are hopeful that this will lead in a direction wherein our interests are fully protected and that there is a complete lifting of restrictions on India that have existed for three decades. Such an outcome if it materializes will contribute to our long-term energy security by enabling a rapid increase in nuclear power. It would lead to the dismantling of the technology denial regimes that have hampered our development particularly in hi-tech sectors. I will have wide consultations including with the members of the Atomic Energy Commission, the nuclear and scientific communities and others to develop a broad based national consensus on this important matter. I wish to inform members of the House that I have invited members of the Atomic Energy Commission on the 26th August for a meeting. That same day I have also invited the group of distinguished scientists who have expressed concerns to meet me.

17. Finally, I would only like to state that in keeping with our commitments to Parliament and the nation, we will not

accept any conditions that go beyond the parameters of the July 18, 2005 Joint Statement and the March 2, 2006 Separation Plan, agreed to between India and the United States. If in their final form the U.S. legislation or the adapted NSG Guidelines impose extraneous conditions on India, the Government will draw the necessary conclusions, consistent with the commitments I have made to Parliament.

[Prime Minister also gave the following responses to points raised by the Left parties]

1. Whether the deal will give "full" civilian nuclear technology and lift all existing sanctions on dual use technology imposed on India for not signing the NPT.

Response: The objective of full civil nuclear cooperation is enshrined in the July Statement. This objective can be realized when current restrictions on nuclear trade with India are fully lifted. In accordance with the July Statement, U.S. has initiated steps to amend its legislation and to approach the NSG to adapt its guidelines. We seek the removal of restrictions on all aspects of cooperation and technology transfers pertaining to civil nuclear energy – ranging from supply of nuclear fuel, nuclear reactors, reprocessing spent fuel, i.e., all aspects of complete nuclear fuel supply. Only such cooperation would be in keeping with the July Joint Statement.

2. Cannot accept restrictions on Indian foreign policy to be imposed such as on Iran, irrespective of whether it is in the policy section or in the sense of the House section of the legislation.

Response: Government is clear that our commitments are only those that are contained in the July Joint Statement and in the Separation Plan. We cannot accept introduction of extraneous issues on foreign policy. Any prescriptive suggestions in this regard are not acceptable to us.

Our foreign policy is and will be solely determined by our national interests. No legislation enacted in a foreign country can take away from us this sovereign right.

3. Signing of IAEA safeguards in perpetuity for the civilian programme to take place after the U.S. Congress had approved

the "123 Nuclear Cooperation Agreement". All restrictions on India to be lifted before we sign the IAEA safeguards.

Response: I had conveyed to Parliament on July 29, 2005 on my return from Washington that before placing any of our nuclear facilities under IAEA safeguards, we will ensure all restrictions on India have been lifted. Under the Separation Plan agreed to with the United States, India has offered to place under IAEA safeguards 14 of its reactors presently operating or under constructions between 2006 and 2014. The nuclear facilities listed in the Separation Plan will be offered for safeguards only after all nuclear restrictions have been lifted on India. This would include suitable amendments to the U.S. legislation to allow for such cooperation, the passing of the bilateral agreement with India and the adaption of the NSG guidelines. It is clear that India cannot be expected to take safeguards obligations on its nuclear facilities in anticipation of future lifting of restrictions.

4. Guarantees on fuel as agreed in the March 2006 statement.

In case the U.S. reneges on supply of fuel, they will ensure continuity through other members of the Nuclear Suppliers Group (NSG).

Response: Separation Plan includes elaborate fuel supply assurances given by the United States. Understandings in the Separation Plan also provide for contingency of disruption of fuel supplies to India. In such a case, the United States and India would jointly convene a group of friendly supplier countries (Russia, France and United Kingdom) aimed at restoring fuel supplies to India. An important assurance is the commitment of support for India's right to build strategic reserves of fuel over the lifetime of its nuclear reactors. In the event of disruption of fuel supplies despite the assurances, India will have a right to take corrective measure to ensure the operation of its nuclear reactors.

5. India will work for an FMCT and for nuclear disarmament with all nuclear weapon states, in line with the Rajiv Gandhi Plan or Delhi Declaration in tandem.

Response: Our support for global nuclear disarmament remains unwaivering. Prime Minister Rajiv Gandhi had put forward an Action Plan in the 1988 UNGA Special Session on Disarmament. We remain committed to the central goal of this Action Plan, i.e., complete elimination of nuclear weapons leading to global nuclear disarmament in a time-bound framework. India has agreed to negotiations in the Conference on Disarmament in Geneva for a Fissile Material Cut-off Treaty. There has been no change in our position on this matter.

6. In the original deal, there is no provision for U.S. inspectors, only provision for IAEA inspectors. The draft U.S. Bill contains such provisions.

Response: In the Separation Plan, we have agreed to offer for IAEA safeguards nuclear facilities specified in the Separation Plan for that purpose. The nature of safeguards will be determined by an India-Specific Safeguards Agreement with the IAEA. This will be applied to the safeguarded nuclear facilities in India. Therefore, there is no question of accepting other verification measures or third country inspectors to visit our nuclear facilities, outside the framework of the India-Specific Safeguards Agreement.

7. An India-specific protocol and not an Additional Protocol as per IAEA Standard Modified Protocol.

Response: In the Separation Plan, we have agreed to conclude an India-Specific Safeguards Agreement with the IAEA. The question of an Additional Protocol will arise only after the India-Specific Safeguards Agreement is in place. As a country with nuclear weapons, there is no question of India agreeing to a safeguards agreement or an Additional Protocol applicable to non-nuclear weapon states of the NPT.

8. References to Iran in the House Bill.

Response: We reject the linkage of any extraneous issue to the nuclear understanding. India's foreign policy will be decided on the basis of Indian national interests only.

9. Reference to Proliferation Security Initiative in the House and Senate Bills.

Response: The Proliferation Security Initiative (PSI) is an extraneous issue as it is outside the framework of the July 18 Joint Statement. Therefore, we cannot accept it as a condition for implementing the July Statement. Separately, the Government has examined the PSI.

We have certain concerns regarding its legal implications and its linkages with the NPT. We also have concerns with amendments to the suppression of Unlawful Activities at Sea Treaty under the International Maritime Organisation.

10. The Jackson-Vanik Amendment linking the granting of MFN status to U.S.S.R. to Jewish emigration is an example relevant to the current debate.

Response: We have studied the proposed U.S. legislation very carefully, including the so-called binding and non-binding provisions. The non-binding provisions do not require mandatory action, but at the same time, have a certain weight in the implementation of the legislation as a whole. We have conveyed our concerns to the U.S. administration in this respect. Jackson-Vanik Amendment was binding on the administration and cannot be cited as a precedent for non-binding references in the current bills. A more accurate example than the Jackson-Vanik Amendment is the set of provisions accompanying the renewal of MFN status to China, that included references to China's human rights, China's political and religious prisoners, protection of Tibetan heritage and freedom of political expression.

11. Role of Parliament in approving foreign policy.

Response: India follows a Parliamentary model, as specified in our Constitution, wherein treaty making powers rest with the Executive. However, we have kept Parliament fully in the picture regarding various stages of our negotiations with the United States. Broad based domestic consensus cutting across all sections in Parliament and outside will be necessary. We will work towards that objective by addressing various concerns as fully as possible.

[Prime Minister also gave the following responses to points raised by the group of nuclear scientists]

1. 'India should continue to be able to hold on to her nuclear option as a strategic requirement in the real world that that we live in, and in the ever-changing complexity of the international political system. This means that we cannot accede to any restraint in perpetuity on our freedom of action. We have not done this for the last 40 years after the Non-Proliferation Treaty came into being, and there is no reason why we should succumb to this now. Universal nuclear disarmament must be our ultimate aim, and until we see the light at the end of the tunnel on this important issue, we cannot accept any agreement in perpetuity.'

Response: We are very firm in our determination that agreement with United States on Civil Nuclear Energy in no way affects the requirements of our strategic program. We are fully conscious of the changing complexity of the international political system. Nuclear weapons are an integral part of our national security and will remain so, pending the global elimination of all nuclear weapons and universal non-discriminatory nuclear disarmament. Our freedom of action with regard to our strategic programs remains unrestricted. The nuclear agreement will not be allowed to be used as a backdoor method of introducing NPT type restrictions on India. Our offer to put nuclear facilities under safeguards in perpetuity is conditional upon these facilities securing fuel from international sources for their lifetime. If the fuel supply assurances as enumerated in Separation Plan are disrupted, then India will have the right to take corrective measures to ensure the continued operation of these reactors.

2. 'After 1974, when the major powers discontinued cooperation with us, we have built up our capability in many sensitive technological areas, which need not and should not now be subjected to external control. Safeguards are understandable where external assistance for nuclear materials or technologies are involved. We have agreed to this before, and we can continue to agree to this in the future too, but strictly

restricted to those facilities and materials imported from external sources.'

Response: Sensitive nuclear technology facilities have not been covered in the Separation Plan. Therefore, there is no question of putting them under safeguards or under external controls. Even with regard to nuclear facilities that have been included in Separation Plan, safeguards will be applied in phases between 2006 and 2014. These safeguarded facilities will be eligible for and will receive fuel materials and technology from international sources. If such supplies cease, then India will be free to protect its interests through corrective measures. That will be spelt out clearly in the India specific safeguards agreement.

3. 'We find that the Indo-U.S. deal, in the form approved by the US House of Representatives, infringes on our independence for carrying out indigenous research and development in nuclear science and technology. Our R&D should not be hampered by external supervision or control, or by the need to satisfy any international body. Research and technology development are the sovereign rights of any nation. This is especially true when they concern strategic national defence and energy self-sufficiency.'

Response: Our independence for carrying out independent research and development in nuclear science and technology will remain unaffected. There will be no external supervision of our R&D since none of the sensitive R&D facilities which handle nuclear material have been included in the Separation Plan. Nothing in the Separation Plan infringes on our sovereign right to conduct research and technology development concerning our national defence and energy self-sufficiency. Government is committed to preserve the integrity of the three stage nuclear power program, including utilization of our vast thorium resources. Certain nuclear facilities including centers such as TIFR, Variable Energy Cyclotron Centre, Saha Institute of Nuclear Physics, etc., have been designated as civilian in the Separation Plan. As these facilities will not handle nuclear material, there is no question of safeguards being applied to them. We expect these centers to participate as full partners in international collaboration project.

4. 'While the sequence of actions to implement the cooperation could be left for discussion between the two governments, the basic principles on which such actions will rest is the right of Parliament and the people to decide. The Prime Minister has already taken up with President George Bush the issue of the new clauses recommended by the U.S. House of Representatives. If the U.S. Congress, in its wisdom, passes the bill in its present form, the 'product' will become unacceptable to India, and diplomatically, it will be very difficult to change it later. Hence, it is important for our Parliament to work out, and insist on, the ground rules for the nuclear deal, at this stage itself.'

Response: I had taken up with President Bush our concerns regarding provisions in the two bills. It is clear that if the final product is in its current form, India will have grave difficulties in accepting the bills. U.S. has been left in no doubt as to our position. The ground rules for our discussions are clear. These are the parameters of the July Statement and the March Separation Plan and commitments given by me to Parliament in the three Suo Moto Statements and my reply to today's discussions will be the guiding principles of our position. Parliament has been kept fully informed at every stage of the discussions. In their final form, if U.S. legislation or the NSG guidelines impose extraneous conditions on India, the Government will draw the necessary conclusions consistent with my commitments to Parliament.

9

President's Statement on House Passage of India Civil Nuclear Cooperation Legislation

July 27, 2006

President Bush commends the House of Representatives for last night's passage of landmark legislation to enable U.S. civil nuclear cooperation with India. This historic action by the House of Representatives is another important step toward building a new strategic partnership between the United States and India, the world's oldest and largest democracies.

The U.S.-India civil nuclear cooperation initiative will help India generate more nuclear power to meet its enormous energy needs in a manner that does not increase greenhouse gas emissions and air pollution, or increase demand on global oil and gas supplies. This initiative also advances U.S. non-proliferation objectives by bringing India into the international non-proliferation mainstream.

The President urges the Senate to act expeditiously to pass companion legislation to enable this important initiative to become a reality.

Rule to Provide for Consideration of H.R. 5682: United States and India Nuclear Cooperation Promotion Act of 2006

10

July 25, 2006

1. Structured rule.

2. Provides one hour of general debate equally divided and controlled by the chairman and ranking minority member of the Committee on International Relations.

3. Waives all points of order against consideration of the bill.

4. Provides that the amendment in the nature of a substitute recommended by the Committee on International Relations now printed in the bill, modified by the amendment printed in part A of the Rules Committee report accompanying the resolution, shall be considered as adopted in the House and in the Committee of the Whole.

5. Provides that the bill, as amended, shall be considered as the original bill for the purpose of further amendment and shall be considered as read.

6. Makes in order only those further amendments printed in part B of the Rules Committee report accompanying the resolution.

7. Provides that the amendments printed in part B of the report may be offered only in the order printed in the report, may be offered only by a Member designated in the report, shall be considered as read, shall be debatable for the time specified in the report equally divided and controlled by the proponent and an opponent, shall not be subject to amendment, and shall not be subject to a demand for division of the question in the House or in the Committee of the Whole.

8. Waives all points of order against the amendments printed in part B of the Rules Committee report.

9. Provides one motion to recommit with or without instructions.

Resolution

Resolved, that at any time after the adoption of this resolution, the Speaker may, pursuant to clause 2(b) of rule XVIII, declare the House resolved into the Committee of the Whole House on the state of the Union for consideration of the bill (H.R. 5682) to exempt from certain requirements of the Atomic Energy Act of 1954 a proposed nuclear agreement for cooperation with India. The first reading of the bill shall be dispensed with. All points of order against consideration of the bill are waived. General debate shall be confined to the bill and shall not exceed one hour equally divided and controlled by the chairman and ranking minority member of the Committee on International Relations. After general debate the bill shall be considered for amendment under the five-minute rule. The amendment in the nature of a substitute recommended by the Committee on International Relations now printed in the bill, modified by the amendment printed in part A of the report of the Committee on Rules accompanying this resolution, shall be considered as adopted in the House and in the Committee of the Whole. The bill, as amended, shall be considered as the original bill for the purpose of further amendment and shall be considered as read. Notwithstanding clause 11 of rule XVIII, no further amendment to the bill, as amended, shall be in order except those printed in part B of the report of the Committee on Rules. Each such amendment may be offered only in the order printed in the report, may be offered only by a Member designated in the report, shall be considered as read, shall be debatable for the time specified in the report equally divided and controlled by the proponent and an opponent, shall not be subject to amendment, and shall not be subject to a demand for division of the question in the House or in the Committee of the Whole. All points of order against such amendments are waived. At the conclusion of consideration of the bill for amendment the Committee shall rise and report the bill, as amended, to the House with such further amendments as may have been adopted. The previous question shall be considered as ordered on the bill and amendments thereto to final passage without intervening motion except one motion to recommit with or without instructions.

Part A - Summary of Amendment Considered as Adopted

The amendment considered as adopted by the rule represents the Committee on Rules' judgment on the matters within its jurisdiction contained in the bill. The amendment states that the joint resolution of approval of a nuclear cooperation agreement between the United States and India shall be considered under the same expedited procedures that a joint resolution of disapproval would be considered for similar cooperation agreements as prescribed by the Nuclear Non-proliferation Provisions of the Atomic Energy Act, including the computation of days as continuous days of session. The amendment preserves the requirement of Congressional approval for the nuclear cooperation agreement.

TEXT OF PART A

Part B - Summary of Amendments Made in Order

(Summaries of amendments derived from information provided by the sponsor)

1. Hyde (IL)/Lantos (CA): Manager's amendment. Contains technical and conforming changes to the text. Also makes one substantive change removing an amendment adopted during the full committee markup relating to subsection 4(b)(7).

2. Stearns (FL): Reinforces the intent of Congress that the nuclear cooperation into which the governments of the United States and India would enter is for peaceful, productive purposes, not military.

3. Jackson-Lee (TX)/Burton (IN): Sense of Congress declaring the importance of the South Asia region and urging the continuation of the United States' policy of engagement, collaboration, and exchanges with and between India and Pakistan.

4. Sherman (CA): Requires that, before any nuclear cooperation with India can go forward, and every year thereafter, the President must certify that during the preceding year India has not increased the level of domestic uranium it sends through its weapons program. Baseline for the determination under the amendment is the 365 day period preceding the July 18, 2005 Bush-Singh declaration on nuclear cooperation.

5. Berman (CA): Restricts exports of uranium and other types of nuclear reactor fuel (defined as "source material" and "special nuclear material" in the Atomic Energy Act of 1954) to India until the President determines that India has halted the production of fissile material (i.e. plutonium and highly enriched uranium) for use in nuclear weapons.

6. Fortenberry (NE): Provides Congress with the ability to assess, to the extent possible, whether annual levels of India's nuclear fissile production may imply a possible violation of Article I of the Nuclear Non-proliferation Treaty.

PART B - TEXT OF THE AMENDMENTS

1. Hyde (IL)/Lantos (CA)
2. Stearns (FL)
3. Jackson-Lee (TX)/Burton (IN)
4. Sherman (CA)
5. Berman (CA)
6. Fortenberry (NE)

Summary of Amendments Submitted to H.R. 5682: United States and India Nuclear Cooperation Promotion Act of 2006

11

July 25, 2006

Berman (CA)

#3 Restricts exports of uranium and other types of nuclear reactor fuel (defined as "source material" and "special nuclear material" in the Atomic Energy Act of 1954) to India until the President determines that India has halted the production of fissile material (i.e. plutonium and highly enriched uranium) for use in nuclear weapons.

Fortenberry (NE)

#4 (2nd Revision) Provides Congress with the ability to assess, to the extent possible, whether annual levels of India's nuclear fissile production may imply a possible violation of Article I of the Nuclear Non-proliferation Treaty (NNPT).

Hyde (IL)/Lantos (CA)

#9 (Withdrawn) Codifies existing practices to protect Congressional prerogatives with respect to arms sales and addresses other Executive/Legislative issues relating to arms sales. Would amend the Arms Export Control Act (AECA) in two areas: (1) Section 3 of the AECA would be amended to require the President to make a written report to Congress within 10 days of receiving information that an unauthorized transfer of U.S. defense articles has been made to a country that is prohibited by law from receiving U.S. defense articles (e.g., Iran, China, etc.). Such a report would have to be made before any new major arms sales are notified to Congress for a country from which such an unauthorized transfer took place; (2) Section 36 of the AECA would be amended to incorporate into law the longstanding practices which have governed the notification of arms sales to Congress: (A) U.S. Government sales (via the Foreign Military Sales program) and commercial sales (via export licensing) are the subject of consultation with congressional staff of HIRC and SFRC before the Executive Branch makes a formal notification to Congress under section 36. Except in rare circumstances, the Executive Branch seeks to resolve any substantive issue identified through these consultations in order to ensure the chairmen and ranking members of both committees have raised no major objections. The President may have this requirement: (1) if there is an emergency or (2) in extraordinary circumstances upon notifying the committees of the circumstances; (B) U.S. Government sales are subject to an additional 20 day advance written notice with respect to countries other than NATO members, Australia, New Zealand and Japan, which account for the majority of exports of U.S. defense articles. The President may also waive this requirement if there is an emergency. In addition, the chairmen and ranking members may have this requirement, as they often do in current practice following the resolution of substantive issues. Would further require the President to consult with the Appropriate Congressional Committees not less than 15 days before an announcement concerning negotiations relating to a new or amended agreement for peaceful nuclear cooperation with another nation.

Hyde (IL)/Lantos (CA)

#10 Manager's Amendment. Contains technical and conforming changes to the text. Also makes one substantive change removing an amendment adopted during the full committee markup relating to subsection 4(b)(7).

Jackson-Lee (TX)/Burton (IN)

#5 Sense of Congress declaring the importance of the South Asia region and urging the continuation of the United States' policy of engagement, collaboration, and exchanges with and between India and Pakistan.

Lee (CA)

#8 (Revised) Would require India to commit to basic provisions consistent with NPT, namely: (1) declare all its civilian nuclear facilities and open them all up for international inspection; (2) undertake a binding obligation not to assist, encourage, or induce non-nuclear weapons states to manufacture or acquire nuclear weapons; and (3) take concrete steps toward disarmament, including drawing down its nuclear stockpile and eventually eliminating all nuclear weapons.

Markey (MA)/Upton (MI)

#7 Requires that nuclear cooperation with India could only commence after the President has determined that the United States has secured India's full and active support in preventing Iran from acquiring weapons of mass destruction.

Sherman (CA)

#2 Requires that, before any nuclear cooperation with India can go forward, and every year thereafter, the President must certify that during the preceding year India has not increased the level of domestic uranium it sends through its weapons program. Baseline for the determination under the amendment is the 365 day period preceding the July 18, 2005 Bush-Singh declaration on nuclear cooperation.

Stearns (FL)

#6 (2nd Revision) Reinforces the intent of Congress that the nuclear cooperation into which the governments of the United States and India would enter is for peaceful, productive purposes, not military.

Woolsey (CA)

#1 Provides that until the President has implemented and observed all NPT obligations and commitments of the United States and has revised U.S. policies relating to nuclear weapons, no item subject to the recent U.S. and India nuclear agreement or the transfer guidelines of the NSG may be transferred to India, including exports of nuclear and nuclear-related material, equipment or technology

Text of H.R. 5682: United States and India Nuclear Cooperation Promotion Act of 2006

12

July 25, 2006

IN THE HOUSE OF REPRESENTATIVES

JUNE 26, 2006

Mr. Hyde (for himself, Mr. Lantos, Ms. Ros-lehtinen, Mr. Ackerman, Mr. Burton of Indiana, Mr. Wilson of South Carolina, Mr. Faleomavaega, Mr. Engel, Mr. Crowley, and Mr. Etheridge) introduced the following bill which was referred to the Committee on International Relations, and in addition to the Committee on Rules, for a period to be subsequently determined by the Speaker, in each case for consideration of such provisions as fall within the jurisdiction of the committee concerned.

JULY 21, 2006

Additional sponsors: Mr. Price of North Carolina, Mr. Miller of North Carolina, Ms. Millender-Mcdonald, Mr. Strickland, Mr. Mcdermott, Mr. King of New York, Mr. Delahunt, Mr. Boustany, Mr. Sessions, Mr. Conaway, Mr. Hall, Mr. Smith of Texas, Mr. Neugebauer, Mr. Carter, Mr. Bonilla, Mr. Foley, Mr. Sam Johnson of Texas, Mr. Linder, Mr. Culberson, Mr. Hensarling, Mr. Mccaul of Texas, Mr. Kolbe, Ms. Granger, Mr. Marchant, Mr. Lewis of Kentucky, and Mr. Miller of Florida.

JULY 21, 2006

Committee on Rules discharged; committed to the Committee of the Whole House on the State of the Union and ordered to be printed.

A BILL

To exempt from certain requirements of the Atomic Energy Act of 1954 a proposed nuclear agreement for cooperation with

India. Be it enacted by the Senate and House of Representatives of the United States of America in Congress assembled.

Section 1. Short Title

This Act may be cited as the "United States and India Nuclear Cooperation Promotion Act of 2006".

Section 2. Sense of Congress

It is the sense of Congress that—

1. preventing the proliferation of nuclear weapons, other weapons of mass destruction, the means to produce them, and the means to deliver them are critical objectives for United States foreign policy;
2. sustaining the NPT and strengthening its implementation, particularly its verification and compliance, is the keystone of United States non-proliferation policy;
3. the NPT has been a significant success in preventing the acquisition of nuclear weapons capabilities and maintaining a stable international security situation;
4. countries that have never become a party to the NPT and remain outside that treaty's legal regime pose a potential challenge to the achievement of the overall goals of global non-proliferation, because those countries have not undertaken the NPT's international obligation to prohibit the spread of dangerous nuclear technologies;
5. it is in the interest of the United States to the fullest extent possible to ensure that those countries that are not NPT members are responsible with any nuclear technology they develop;
6. it may be in the interest of the United States to enter into an agreement for nuclear cooperation as set forth in section 123 of the Atomic Energy Act of 1954 (42 U.S.C. 2153) with a country that has never been an NPT member with respect to civilian nuclear technology if—

    (A) the country has demonstrated responsible behavior with respect to the non-proliferation of technology related to weapons of mass destruction programs and the means to deliver them;

(B) the country has a functioning and uninterrupted democratic system of government, has a foreign policy that is congruent to that of the United States, and is working with the United States in key foreign policy initiatives related to non-proliferation;

(C) such cooperation induces the country to implement the highest possible protections against the proliferation of technology related to weapons of mass destruction programs and the means to deliver them, and to refrain from actions that would further the development of its nuclear weapons program; and

(D) such cooperation will induce the country to give greater political and material support to the achievement of United States' global and regional non-proliferation objectives, especially with respect to dissuading, isolating, and, if necessary, sanctioning and containing states that sponsor terrorism and terrorist groups, that are seeking to acquire a nuclear weapons capability or other weapons of mass destruction capability and the means to deliver such weapons; and

7. (A) India meets the criteria described in this subsection; and

   (B) it is in the national security interest of the United States to deepen its relationship with India across a full range of issues, including peaceful nuclear cooperation.

Section 3. Statements Of Policy

(a) In General—The following shall be the policies of the United States:

1. Oppose the development of a capability to produce nuclear weapons by any non-nuclear weapon state, within or outside of the Treaty on the Non-Proliferation

of Nuclear Weapons (21 UST 483; commonly referred to as the "Nuclear Non-proliferation Treaty" or the "NPT").

2. Encourage states party to the NPT to interpret the right to "develop research, production and use of nuclear energy for peaceful purposes", as described in Article IV of the NPT, as being a qualified right that is conditioned by the overall purpose of the NPT to prevent the spread of nuclear weapons and nuclear weapons capability, including by refraining from all nuclear cooperation with any state party that has not demonstrated that it is in full compliance with its NPT obligations, as determined by the IAEA.

3. Strengthen the Nuclear Suppliers Group guidelines concerning consultation by members regarding violations of supplier and recipient understandings by instituting the practice of a timely and coordinated response by NSG members to all such violations, including termination of nuclear transfers to an involved recipient, that discourages individual NSG members from continuing cooperation with such recipient until such time as a consensus regarding a coordinated response has been achieved.

(b) With Respect to South Asia—The following shall be the policies of the United States with respect to South Asia:

1. Achieve a moratorium on the production of fissile material for nuclear explosive purposes by India, Pakistan, and the People's Republic of China at the earliest possible date.

2. Achieve, at the earliest possible date, the conclusion and implementation of a treaty banning the production of fissile material for nuclear weapons to which both the United States and India become parties.

3. Secure India's—

(A) full participation in the Proliferation Security Initiative;

(B) formal commitment to the Statement of Interdiction Principles;

(C) public announcement of its decision to conform its export control laws, regulations, and policies with the Australia Group and with the Guidelines, Procedures, Criteria, and Control Lists of the Wassennaar Arrangement;

(D) demonstration of satisfactory progress toward implementing the decision described in subparagraph (C); and

(E) ratification of or accession to the Convention on Supplementary Compensation for Nuclear Damage, done at Vienna on September 12, 1997.

4. Secure India's full and active participation in United States efforts to dissuade, isolate, and, if necessary, sanction and contain Iran for its efforts to acquire weapons of mass destruction, including a nuclear weapons capability (including the capability to enrich or process nuclear materials), and the means to deliver weapons of mass destruction.
5. Seek to halt the increase of nuclear weapon arsenals in South Asia, and to promote their reduction and eventual elimination.
6. To ensure that spent fuel generated in India's civilian nuclear power reactors is not transferred to the United States except pursuant to the Congressional review procedures required under section 131 f. of the Atomic Energy Act of 1954 (42 U.S.C. 2160 f.).
7. Pending implementation of a multilateral moratorium, encourage India not to increase its production of fissile material at unsafeguarded nuclear facilities.

Section 4. Waiver Authority and Congressional Approval

(a) In General—Notwithstanding any other provision of law, if the President makes the determination described in subsection (b), the President may—

1. exempt a proposed agreement for nuclear cooperation with India (arranged pursuant to section 123 of the Atomic Energy Act of 1954 (42 U.S.C. 2153)) from the requirement in section 123 a.(2) of such Act, and such agreement for cooperation may only enter into force in accordance with subsections (f) and (g);
2. waive the application of section 128 of the Atomic Energy Act of 1954 (42 U.S.C. 2157) with respect to India, provided that such waiver shall cease to be effective if the President determines that India has engaged in any activity described in section 129 of such Act (42 U.S.C. 2158), other than section 129 a.(1)(D) or section 129 a.(2)(C) of such Act, at any time after the date of the enactment of this Act; and
3. with respect to India—
   (A) waive the restrictions of section 129 a.(1)(A) of the Atomic Energy Act of 1954 (42 U.S.C. 2158 a.(1)(A)) for any activity that occurred on or before July 18, 2005; and

   (B) section 129 a.(1)(D) of such Act.

(b) Determination by the President—The determination referred to in subsection (a) is a determination by the President that the following actions have occurred:

1. India has provided the United States and the International Atomic Energy Agency with a credible plan to separate civil and military nuclear facilities, materials, and programs, and has filed a declaration regarding its civil facilities with the IAEA.
2. India and the IAEA have concluded an agreement requiring the application of IAEA safeguards in perpetuity in accordance with IAEA standards, principles, and practices (including IAEA Board of Governors Document GOV/1621 (1973)) to India's civil nuclear facilities, materials, and programs as declared in the plan described in paragraph (1), including materials used in or produced through the use of India's civil nuclear facilities.

3. India and the IAEA are making substantial progress toward concluding an Additional Protocol consistent with IAEA principles, practices, and policies that would apply to India's civil nuclear program.
4. India is working actively with the United States for the early conclusion of a multilateral Fissile Material Cut-off Treaty.
5. India is working with and supporting United States and international efforts to prevent the spread of enrichment and reprocessing technology.
6. India is taking the necessary steps to secure nuclear and other sensitive materials and technology, including through—
   (A) the enactment and enforcement of comprehensive export control legislation and regulations;
   (B) harmonization of its export control laws, regulations, policies, and practices with the policies and practices of the Missile Technology Control Regime and the Nuclear Suppliers Group; and
   (C) adherence to the MTCR and the NSG in accordance with the procedures of those regimes for unilateral adherence.
7. The NSG has decided by consensus to permit supply to India of nuclear items covered by the guidelines of the NSG and such decision does not permit civil nuclear commerce with any other non-nuclear weapon state that does not have IAEA safeguards on all nuclear materials within its territory, under its jurisdiction, or carried out under its control anywhere.

(c) Submission to Congress—

1. In General—The President shall submit to the Committee on International Relations of the House of Representatives and the Committee on Foreign Relations of the Senate information concerning any determination made pursuant to subsection (b), together with a report detailing the basis for the determination.

2. Information to be Included—To the fullest extent available to the United States, the information referred to in paragraph (1) shall include the following:

(A) A summary of the plan provided by India to the United States and the IAEA to separate India's civil and military nuclear facilities, materials, and programs, and the declaration made by India to the IAEA identifying India's civil facilities to be placed under IAEA safeguards, including an analysis of the credibility of such plan and declaration, together with copies of the plan and declaration.

(B) A summary of the agreement that has been entered into between India and the IAEA requiring the application of safeguards in accordance with IAEA practices to India's civil nuclear facilities as declared in the plan described in subparagraph (A), together with a copy of the agreement, and a description of the progress toward its full implementation.

(C) A summary of the progress made toward conclusion and implementation of an Additional Protocol between India and the IAEA, including a description of the scope of such Additional Protocol.

(D) A description of the steps that India is taking to work with the United States for the conclusion of a multilateral treaty banning the production of fissile material for nuclear weapons, including a description of the steps that the United States has taken and will take to encourage India to identify and declare a date by which India would be willing to stop production of fissile material for nuclear weapons unilaterally or pursuant to a multilateral moratorium or treaty.

(E) A description of the steps India is taking to prevent the spread of nuclear-related technology, including enrichment and reprocessing technology or materials that can be used to acquire a nuclear weapons technology, as well as the support that India is providing to the United States to further United States' objectives to restrict the spread of such technology.

(F) A description of the steps that India is taking to secure materials and technology applicable for the development, acquisition, or manufacture of weapons of mass destruction and the means to deliver such weapons through the application of comprehensive export control legislation and regulations, and through harmonization and adherence to Missile Technology Control Regime, the Nuclear Suppliers Group, the Australia Group, Wassennaar guidelines, and United Nations Security Council Resolution 1540, and participation in the Proliferation Security Initiative.

(G) A description of the decision taken within the Nuclear Suppliers Group relating to nuclear cooperation with India, including whether nuclear cooperation by the United States under an agreement for cooperation arranged pursuant to section 123 of the Atomic Energy Act of 1954 (42 U.S.C. 2153) is consistent with the decision, practices, and policies of the NSG.

(H) A description of the scope of peaceful cooperation envisioned by the United States and India that will be implemented under the Agreement for Nuclear Cooperation, including whether such cooperation will include the provision of enrichment and reprocessing technology.

(I) A description of the steps taken to ensure that proposed United States civil nuclear assistance to India will not directly, or in any other way, assist India's nuclear weapons program, including—

(i) the use of any United States' equipment, technology, or nuclear material by India in an unsafeguarded nuclear facility or nuclear-weapons related complex;

(ii) the replication and subsequent use of any United States technology in an unsafeguarded nuclear facility or unsafeguarded nuclear weapons-related complex, or for any activity related to the research, development, testing, or manufacture of nuclear explosive devices; and

(iii) the provision of nuclear fuel in such a manner as to facilitate the increased production of highly-enriched uranium or plutonium in unsafeguarded nuclear facilities.

(d) Restrictions on Nuclear Transfers to India—

1. In General—Pursuant to the obligations of the United States under Article I of the NPT, nothing in this Act, or any agreement pursuant to this Act, shall be interpreted as permitting any civil nuclear cooperation between the United States and India that would in any way assist, encourage, or induce India to manufacture or otherwise acquire nuclear weapons or nuclear explosive devices.
2. NSG Transfer Guidelines—Notwithstanding the entry into force of an agreement for cooperation with India pursuant to section 123 of the Atomic Energy Act of 1954 (42 U.S.C. 2153) and approved pursuant to this Act, no item subject to such agreement or subject to the transfer guidelines of the NSG may be transferred to India if such transfer would violate the transfer guidelines of the NSG as in effect on the date of the transfer.
3. Termination of Nuclear Transfers to India—Notwithstanding the entry into force of an agreement for nuclear cooperation with India (arranged pursuant to section 123 of the Atomic Energy Act of 1954 (42 U.S.C. 2153)), exports of nuclear and nuclear-related material, equipment, or technology to India shall be terminated if India makes any materially significant transfer of—

(A) nuclear or nuclear-related material, equipment, or technology that does not conform to NSG guidelines, or

(B) ballistic missiles or missile-related equipment or technology that does not conform to MTCR guidelines, unless the President determines that cessation of such exports would be seriously prejudicial to the achievement of United States non-proliferation objectives or otherwise jeopardize the common defense and security.

4. Prohibition on Nuclear Transfers to India—If nuclear transfers to India are restricted pursuant to this Act, the Atomic Energy Act of 1954, or the Arms Export Control Act, the President should seek to prevent the transfer to India of nuclear equipment, materials, or technology from other participating governments in the NSG or from any other source.

(e) Approval of Agreement for Nuclear Cooperation Required—

1. In General—Subject to subsection (m), an agreement for nuclear cooperation between the United States and India submitted pursuant to this section may become effective only if—

(A) the President submits to Congress the agreement concluded between the United States and India, including a copy of the safeguards agreement entered into between the IAEA and India relating to India's declared civilian nuclear facilities, in accordance with the requirements and procedures of section 123 of the Atomic Energy Act of 1954 (other than section 123 a.(2) of such Act) that are otherwise not inconsistent with the provisions of this Act; and

(B) after the submission under subparagraph (A), the agreement is approved by a joint resolution that is enacted into law.

2. Consultation—Beginning one month after the date of the enactment of this Act and every month thereafter until the President submits to Congress the agreement referred to in paragraph (1), the President should consult with the Committee on International Relations of the House of Representatives and the Committee on Foreign Relations of the Senate regarding the status of the negotiations between the United States and India with respect to civilian nuclear cooperation and between the IAEA and India with respect to the safeguards agreement described in subsection (b) (2).

(f) Joint Resolution—For purposes of this section, a joint resolution referred to in subsection (e)(1)(B) is a joint resolution of the two Houses of Congress—

1. the matter after the resolving clause of which is as follows: "That the Congress hereby approves the Agreement for Nuclear Cooperation Between the United States of America and the Republic of India submitted by the President on.", with the blank space being filled with the appropriate date;
2. which does not have a preamble; and
3. the title of which is as follows: "Joint Resolution Approving an Agreement for Nuclear Cooperation Between the United States and India".

(g) Introduction And Referral—

1. Introduction—A joint resolution shall, on the day on which the submissions under subsection (e)(1)(A) are made (or, if either House of Congress is not in session on that day, the first day thereafter when that House is in session)—

(A) be introduced in the House of Representatives by the majority leader, for himself and the minority leader of the House, or by Members of the House designated by the majority leader and minority leader of the House; and

(B) be introduced in the Senate by the majority leader, for himself and the minority leader of the Senate, or by Members of the Senate designated by the majority leader and minority leader of the Senate.

If either House of Congress is not in session on that day, the joint resolution shall be introduced on the first day thereafter when both Houses are in session.

2. Referral—The joint resolution shall be referred to the Committee on International Relations of the House of Representatives and to the Committee on Foreign Relations of the Senate.

(h) Discharge of Committees—If a committee to which a joint resolution is referred has not reported such joint resolution by the end of 60 days beginning on the date of its introduction, or the date of the submission of the non-proliferation assessment statement described in section 123 of the Atomic Energy Act of 1954 (42 U.S.C. 2153), whichever is later, such committee shall be discharged from further consideration of such joint resolution, and such joint resolution shall be placed on the appropriate calendar of the House involved.

(i) Floor Consideration in the House of Representatives—

1. In General—On or after the third calendar day (excluding Saturdays, Sundays, or legal holidays, except when the House of Representatives is in session on such a day) after the date on which the committee to which a joint resolution is referred has reported, or has been discharged from further consideration of, such a joint resolution, it shall be in order for any Member of the House to move to proceed to the consideration of the joint resolution. A Member of the House may make the motion only on the day after the calendar day on which the Member announces to the House the Member's intention to do so. Such motion shall be privileged and shall not be debatable. The motion shall not be subject to amendment or to a motion to postpone. A motion to reconsider the vote by which the motion is agreed to shall not be in order. If a motion to proceed to the

consideration of the joint resolution is agreed to, the House shall immediately proceed to consideration of the joint resolution which shall remain the unfinished business until disposed of.

2. Debate—Debate on a joint resolution, and on all debatable motions and appeals in connection therewith, shall be limited to not more than six hours, which shall be divided equally between those favoring and those opposing the joint resolution. An amendment to the joint resolution shall not be in order. A motion to further limit debate shall be in order and shall not be debatable. A motion to table, a motion to postpone, or a motion to recommit the joint resolution shall not be in order. A motion to reconsider the vote by which the joint resolution is agreed to or disagreed to shall not be in order.
3. Appeals—Appeals from the decisions of the Chair to the procedure relating to a joint resolution shall be decided without debate.

(j) Floor Consideration in the Senate—Any joint resolution shall be considered in the Senate in accordance with the provisions of section 601(b)(4) of the International Security Assistance and Arms Export Control Act of 1976.

(k) Consideration by the other House—If, before the passage by one House of a joint resolution of that House, that House receives a joint resolution from the other House, then the following procedures shall apply:

1. The joint resolution of the other House shall not be referred to a committee and may not be considered in the House receiving it except in the case of final passage as provided in paragraph (2)(B).
2. With respect to a joint resolution of the House receiving the joint resolution—
   - (A) the procedure in that House shall be the same as if no joint resolution had been received from the other House; but

(B) the vote on final passage shall be on the joint resolution of the other House.

3. Upon disposition of the joint resolution received from the other House, it shall no longer be in order to consider the joint resolution that originated in the receiving House.

(l) Computation of Days—In the computation of the period of 60 days referred to in subsection (h), there shall be excluded the days on which either House of Congress is not in session because of an adjournment of more than 3 days to a day certain or because of an adjournment of the Congress *sine die*.

(m) Section 123 of Atomic Energy Act of 1954 Not Affected—Notwithstanding subsection (e)(1), this section does not preclude the approval, under section 123 of the Atomic Energy Act of 1954 (42 U.S.C. 2153), of an agreement for cooperation in which India is the cooperating party.

(n) Sunset—The procedures under this section shall cease to be effective upon the enactment of a joint resolution under this section.

(o) Reports—

1. Policy Objectives—The President shall, not later than January 31, 2007, and not later than January 31 of each year thereafter, submit to the Committee on International Relations of the House of Representatives and the Committee on Foreign Relations of the Senate a report on—

(A) the extent to which each policy objective in section 3(b) has been achieved;

(B) the steps taken by the United States and India in the preceding calendar year to accomplish those objectives;

(C) the extent of cooperation by other countries in achieving those objectives; and

(D) the steps the United States will take in the current calendar year to accomplish those objectives.

2. Nuclear Exports to India—
   (A) In General—Not later than one year after the date on which an agreement for nuclear cooperation between the United States and India is approved by Congress under section (f) and every year thereafter, the President shall submit to the Committee on International Relations of the House of Representatives and the Committee on Foreign Relations of the Senate a report describing United States' exports to India for the preceding year pursuant to such agreement and the anticipated exports to India for the next year pursuant to such agreement.
   (B) Nuclear Fuel—The report described in subparagraph (A) shall also include (in a classified form if necessary)—
      (i) an estimate for the previous year of the amount of uranium mined in India;
      (ii) the amount of such uranium that has likely been used or allocated for the production of nuclear explosive devices;
      (iii) the rate of production of—
         (I) fissile material for nuclear explosive devices; and
         (II) nuclear explosive devices; and
      (iv) an analysis as to whether imported uranium has affected such rate of production of nuclear explosive devices.
   (C) Unsafeguarded Nuclear Facilities—The report described in subparagraph (A) shall also include (in a classified form if necessary) a description of whether United States' civil nuclear assistance to India is directly, or in any other way, assisting India's nuclear weapons program, including—

(i) the use of any United States' equipment, technology, or nuclear material by India in an unsafeguarded nuclear facility or nuclear-weapons related complex;

(ii) the replication and subsequent use of any United States technology in an unsafeguarded nuclear facility or unsafeguarded nuclear weapons-related complex, or for any activity related to the research, development, testing, or manufacture of nuclear explosive devices; and

(iii) the provision of nuclear fuel in such a manner as to facilitate the increased production of highly-enriched uranium or plutonium in unsafeguarded nuclear facilities.

3. New Nuclear Reactors or Facilities—Not later than one year after the date of the enactment of this Act and annually thereafter, the President shall submit to the Committee on International Relations of the House of Representatives and the Committee on Foreign Relations of the Senate a report describing any new nuclear reactors or nuclear facilities that the Government of India has designated as civilian and placed under inspections or has designated as military.

4. Disposal of Spent Nuclear Fuel—Not later than one year after the date on which an agreement for nuclear cooperation between the United States and India is approved by Congress under section 4(f) and every year thereafter, the President shall submit to the Committee on International Relations of the House of Representatives and the Committee on Foreign Relations of the Senate a report describing the disposal of spent nuclear fuel from India's civilian nuclear program.

(p) Definitions—In this Act:

1. IAEA—The term "IAEA" means the International Atomic Energy Agency.

2. MTCR—The term "MTCR" means the Missile Technology Control Regime.

3. NPT—The term "NPT" means the Treaty on the Non-proliferation of Nuclear Weapons.
4. NPT MEMBER—The term "NPT member" means a country that is a party to the NPT.
5. NSG—The term "NSG" means the Nuclear Suppliers Group.

Lok Sabha Starred Question No. 373 Answered On 10.05.2006

13

Shri Tathagata Satpathy
Shri Chandra Bhushan Singh
May 10, 2006

Will the Prime Minister be pleased to state: (a) whether the U.S. asked India to ban nuclear tests permanently as part of Indo-U.S. nuclear deal as per the draft agreement received in this regard; b) if so, the details thereof; and c) the response of the Union Government thereto?

Answer—The Minister of State in The Ministry of External Affairs (Shri Anand Sharma)

(a)-(b) Discussions are ongoing between India and the United States on a bilateral civil nuclear energy cooperation agreement. Among the elements in the draft proposed by the United States, there was a reference to cooperation being discontinued were India to detonate a nuclear explosive device.

(c) India has conveyed to the United States that such a provision has no place in the proposed bilateral agreement and that India is bound only by its commitment in the July 18, 2005 Joint Statement to continuing a unilateral moratorium on nuclear testing.

Relevant Extract of the "Glenn Amendment" on Sanctions:

Amendment to the Arms Export Control Act

(b) prohibitions on assistance to countries involved in transfer or use of nuclear explosive devices; exceptions; procedures applicable—

(1) Except as provided in paragraphs (4), (5), and (6), in the event that the President determines that any country, after the

effective date of part B of the Nuclear Proliferation Prevention Act of 1994—

(A) transfers to a non-nuclear-weapon state a nuclear explosive device;

(B) is a non-nuclear-weapon state and either--

(i) receives a nuclear explosive device, or

(ii) detonates a nuclear explosive device;

(C) transfers to a non-nuclear-weapon state any design information or component which is determined by the President to be important to, and known by the transferring country to be intended by the recipient state for use in, the development or manufacture of any nuclear explosive device; or

(D) is a non-nuclear-weapon state and seeks and receives any design information or component which is determined by the President to be important to, and intended by the recipient state for use in, the development or manufacture of any nuclear explosive device, then the President shall forthwith report in writing his determination to the Congress and shall forthwith impose the sanctions described in paragraph (2) against that country.

Text of statement made by MEA Spokesman (17 April 2006)

"U.S. has shared with India some weeks ago a preliminary draft Agreement on the Indo-U.S. civil nuclear cooperation under article 123 of the U.S. Atomic Energy Act. Among the elements suggested by the United States there is a reference to cooperation being discontinued were India to detonate a nuclear explosive device. In the preliminary discussions on these elements so far India has already conveyed to the United States that such a provision has no place in the proposed bilateral agreement and that India is bound only by what is contained in the July 18 Joint Statement, that is continuing its commitment to a unilateral moratorium on nuclear testing. India's position on CTBT, that you mentioned, is well-known and continues to remain valid."

Relevant Text of the Draft Bilateral Agreement

Article 11 - Cessation of Cooperation

1. If either Party at any time following entry into force of this Agreement:

(A) does not comply with the provisions of Article 5, 6, 7, 8, or 9; or

(B) terminates, abrogates, or materially violates a safeguards agreement with the IAEA, the other Party shall have the rights to cease further cooperation under this Agreement and to require the return of any material, equipment, or components transferred under this Agreement and any special nuclear material and weapons-usable byproduct material produced through their use.

2. If India at any time following entry into force of this Agreement detonates a nuclear explosive device, the United States of America shall have the same rights as specified in paragraph l.

3. If either Party exercises its rights under this Article to require the return of any material, equipment, or components it shall, after removal from the territory of the other Party, reimburse the other Party for the fair market value of such material, equipment, or components.

The U.S.-India Friendship: Where We Were and Where We're Going

14

Richard A. Boucher, Assistant Secretary for South and Central Asian Affairs

April 7, 2006

....If we can come to an agreement on civil-nuclear cooperation—and we did after struggling with the issue for 30 years—we can do anything.

I am happy to report that since the announcement, both sides have worked hard towards fulfilling their commitments. Just this week, Dr. Anil Kakodkar, the Chairman of India's Atomic Energy Commission, travelled to Vienna to begin discussions with the IAEA on a safeguards agreement, and Secretary Rice testified before both Houses of the U.S. Congress in support of this initiative, declaring it to be the key element of "a partnership that will become one of the most important we have with any country in the 21st century".

As Secretary Rice said, this initiative "is a strategic achievement. It will strengthen international security. It will enhance energy security and environmental protection. It will foster economic and technological development. And it will help further transform the partnership between the world's oldest and the world's largest democracy." Delivering on our many commitments will take work by both sides—diplomatically, domestically and bureaucratically. As we transform our relationship, we must transform our attitudes and structures. America's growing stake in India's future means that we will continue to talk frankly with you as friends do with one another about economic reform. And we expect that you'll continue to offer us pointers on things we could do better, as all of our best friends in the world do... .

....As in the past, we continue to look to India for leadership in stabilizing nuclear and defense relations with its neighbors. We, and previous American Administrations, have pushed for India to further define its "minimum credible deterrent", and we continue that today. We understand the complexity of this task having spent 40 years in discussions with the former Soviet Union over our nuclear weapons programs. We also understand that such discussions are complicated by China's intentions and by Iran's energetic pursuit of technologies that underlie nuclear weapons. But, nevertheless, we see this as an absolutely necessary step toward decreasing tensions in Asia. We look not only to India, but to Pakistan, to work out mutual understandings to build confidence in both conventional and nuclear areas.

In addition to working bilaterally with India, we see great promise in working together in the South Asian Association for Regional Cooperation (SAARC). We recently approached SAARC's Secretary General requesting observer status. South Asian Free Trade is an opportunity for all the countries of South Asia to help make free trade in the region a reality, and to establish links to Central Asian economic organizations....

Question: Professor Rasha Bramanin, [inaudible] University. If I may, Ambassador, come to the knotty problem of the Indo-U.S. civilian nuclear cooperation.

Assistant Secretary Boucher: How do spell that word, knotty? [Laughter].

Question: Well, I leave it to you.

Assistant Secretary Boucher: Is it naughty or knotty? Either one.

Question: I am a nuclear physicist trained in the United States' most premier universities—Harvard, Stanford, Berkeley. So I know a little bit about nuclear physics, not too much about politics. But your Congress is facing election, our Congress may face election, I don't know. But the specific issue is here, from what it appears now it's gone beyond the administration to your legislative branch and there are compulsions which seem to suggest, looking at it, I mean I rely on the press, I have no access to government or its information. There is a definite problem.

It's all very well to say our non-proliferation record is impeccable, but the enshrinement and edification called the Non-Proliferation Treaty is basically what is related to your own congressional act of 1978, amendment to the Atomic Energy Act.

Now where does this act leave us right now? We have considered 60 per cent of the facilities. The administration has been very forthcoming. I personally tend to agree with you, there are many more issues that are going on in the economic front, defense relationship and so on. The nuclear has always been a knotty problem. It seems to have surfaced again. The Democrats, given their capacity for non-proliferation and so on.

Can you please tell me what is the state, or what is the likelihood? Because the NSG is looking. It's all very well for the Chairman of the Atomic Energy to seek India specific safeguards, but everyone is waiting for this deal to go through. Can you please tell me, will this deal go through or not? Yes or no? Thank you, sir.

Assistant Secretary Boucher: Yes. [Laughter]. Next question. [Laughter].

I still think the answer is yes. The Secretary of State was out in public yesterday two times for two hours each at least, up in front of Congress, going through the process of democracy. It's noisy and it's messy and there are lots of things said about you and there's lots of things said about me that we don't like and don't agree with, but that's democracy and you guys know it as well as we do.

I think it's going to go through for some fundamental reasons. This is part and parcel of a new relationship with India and I think people want to support that relationship. It's part and parcel of meeting the energy needs, the growing energy needs of a growing economy without putting more pressure on fossil fuels and oil prices which is in all our interests, all of us who drive cars. And it's part and parcel of, in a way, stabilizing this region of the world. The net improvement in non-proliferation around the world we think is clear.

There are serious questions involved here, though. I don't deny the critics their day. I think they have raised a lot of things that need to be discussed for us and for you. Non-proliferation has always been done through the Non-Proliferation Treaty. The rules, the procedures, the mindset is all based on the Non-Proliferation Treaty. It took us a while to figure out that it was worth it to do the deal with India that was you might say is alongside the practices that we had based on the treaty. And I think it takes critics and people who are concerned about non-proliferation a little while to think these things through, to look at all the aspects, to look at all the implications. Does it undercut the treaty? Does it lead to greater production on the military side? Does it change the rules for future candidates? Does it somehow change the rules for India in a way that is a disincentive to restraint and confidence building in these areas?

Those are serious questions. I think we've answered them as well as we can. I think we've answered them fully and forthrightly for our Congress and for the many groups that we've seen. We've gone out to talk to business groups and universities and academics and experts and scholars and a lot of people who are involved in this discussion. But I think in the end people want to support the new relationship with India. They will agree this is a net positive for the non-proliferation effort that we're all making around the world. And that it will pass.

So yesterday you saw a number of Senators and Congressmen declare their support. Some of them sort of declared their support. Others kind of sort of declared their support. But that's a gradual process for some. There are some serious questions that everybody needs to think about and I think the momentum is positive.

Question: Sir, can you talk about [inaudible]? Is this not a potential deal-breaker? And if not, why so?

Assistant Secretary Boucher: I don't think it's a demand. I think it's something we've always encouraged that we would continue to encourage. As any nation embarks upon a military policy, tries to design its structure of forces and its quantity of forces, it has to have a doctrine, it has to have a way of tying the doctrine to the needs in terms of actual equipment. I think that applies in the area of nuclear weapons as well. So it's hard to define what the future of nuclear weapons in this part of the world is and how countries in this region could reach stability. I think without some more thinking and discussion of some of these concepts. But that's something we would encourage. That's what I said in there. I didn't say it was a new requirement or anything. We're proceeding with the deal and we're proceeding with many other things in our relationship including a discussion of these areas where we think they deserve to be spelled out a little more....

Question: Ambassador, thank you for that wonderful presentation. You referred to China, and quite rightly I think, used the wonderful phrase that it cannot and should not be a zero sum game between China, the United States and India. However, we have had a serious history of problems with China and we have done a great deal, the Indian system has done a great deal to improve relationships, the border talks, the trade relations, etc. And many analysts believe that Indian foreign policy challenge today or in the coming decade will really be to manage the growing relationship with the United States and the improving relationship with China. And that is where some finessing would have to be done.

In the light of it, in relation to the Indo-U.S. nuclear relationship, what is the consultative process you have with the Chinese who are definitely going to take a strong position on it? And how do you see this unfolding? Thank you.

Assistant Secretary Boucher: Let me say, I've worked on China all my life and realize not everything is smooth sailing with the Chinese. What was the phrase you used, we have had some difficult periods in our relationships with China too. And we remember your history and ours as well in terms of relations with China for the last few decades. At the same time I think there are real opportunities opening up. Our goal is to get China to become a responsible stakeholder in the international system, that is a responsible power that abides by the various rules, whether they're export rules or import rules, WTO rules, control of technology rules, human rights rules, the responsibilities of Security Council membership and other things like that. So we're looking for China to become a responsible stakeholder in these international institutions, and sometimes it's rocky and sometimes it's smooth.

I think the course with India will be somewhat smoother as we go forward because we share a lot more in common, including democracy and people and families and education systems and other things with India.

How does China play in this civil nuclear deal? China is a major member of the IAEA and the Nuclear Suppliers Group. So as one of the countries there we are talking to them, working with them. When I went out to Vienna with one of my colleagues we met with a lot of countries, some of them small groups, big groups, but we certainly spent some time talking to the Chinese. I expect I'll continue talking to the Chinese as time goes forward as a member of the Nuclear Suppliers Group who we expect to take a responsible position on these issues.

I think in the end, I've watched India-China relationships a little bit in the last few years, and it seems to me both sides recognize the economic potential of the other, the potential for interaction as well as competition. That's fine. Opportunities. I'm struck by the number of Indian companies that have invested in China. So I don't see any reason why China should think that using this method to provide the energy that India needs to grow, that there's anything wrong with that. So we're hopeful.

Question: [Inaudible].

Assistant Secretary Boucher: Are you a member of the press?

Question: [Inaudible].

Assistant Secretary Boucher: I'm sorry, but I really came to talk to these folks. I'm glad you're here, but I think we're going to let them ask the questions, okay?

Question: Secretary Boucher, thank you very much for your quick presentation on the most salient points that are really exercising many of us in this region. There are two quick questions that I have, and one is perhaps something that I probably missed. You did say something about non-proliferation and the division between the specialists and the regionalists. In a kind of way you referred to that both within the Congress and within the administration. I guess that's what you mean when you said transforming structure and the mindsets, probably. But I'm also interested in your views on cooperation on counter-proliferation because it seems to me that the question of non-proliferation and cooperating with India involves a lot more than just this deal. It would mean India coming on board, for example, on the PSI on which I think there has been a history of differences and we need to be a little more....

Then the question of dovetailing the Iran question. Why has that become such an important and elevated issue all the time? We have an independent policy. We continue to express our policies and our reservations on issues. Why has it become such an important thing in this whole thing? Thank you.

Assistant Secretary Boucher: That's a lot there. Let me try to take it in order.

I don't think the debate in the United States divides up too easily. I made a sweeping generalization about the need to change attitudes and structures across the relationship. That applies to all of us. It does apply somewhat to the nuclear issue. But I've seen Democrats come out for this agreement, I've seen Republicans come out for this agreement, I've seen Democrats oppose it. I'm not sure I've seen Republicans oppose it at this point, but anyway. I've seen people who have worked long and hard on strategic issues academically, on non-proliferation issues support the agreement and oppose the agreement. Some of the people I've talked to who know far more than me about these things have studied it carefully and come out one way or the other.

It is a kind of on-balance judgment that we all make. Is it on-balance good, is it on-balance bad? It's not the perfect deal. But we don't hide the fact that we would have loved to have India abandon its nuclear weapons and join the Non-Proliferation Treaty. That would have been fine by us. We were realistic enough to know that wasn't going to happen. I'm sure India would have been happy to join the Non-Proliferation Treaty as a nuclear weapons state. I'm sure India was realistic enough to know that wasn't going to happen. So we both got to a deal that was on-balance good for us and that's where we ended up, so I think that's the important part.

That's where I'm going to have to stop.

Question: Thank you for recognizing me. What I want to ask you, Ambassador is, is there a time-frame to this agreement, this deal? When do you expect it to be passed? And are you asking India to revise a bit of its earlier position on certain issues which are of particular concern to the United States? Thank you.

Assistant Secretary Boucher: We'll always ask India to revise its position on particular issues that are of concern to the United States. It's up to India whether it does it or not. But we're not asking for other revisions or changes in the context of this deal. We've made very clear to a lot of people that we've negotiated what we think is the best deal that's available at this point, that does the right thing for us, for India, for non-proliferation, for energy needs. We're not going to renegotiate it, we're not going to accept conditions that require renegotiation. That doesn't mean we've abandoned all or other positions and things we'd like to talk to the Indian government about, nor does it mean frankly the Indian government has abandoned its positions and things it wants to talk to us about.

I think the simple answer is we're full speed ahead at this point. We're looking for a vote in Congress if we can, as soon as they can arrange it. I hesitate to predict Congress because they do set their own schedule and they don't listen to us, and they're very hard to judge sometimes, but they're dealing with it. They're having hearings. They had the Secretary up. They're having other hearings. They are actually working this thing fairly smoothly in the halls of Congress, and I hope we'll get a vote a few months from now.

But let's all remember, there's a lot of pieces to this puzzle that have to be fit together. One is the congressional vote from the U.S. side. Another is the approval by the Nuclear Suppliers

Group. Another is the Safeguards Agreement that India negotiates with the International Atomic Energy Agency. And another is the bilateral agreement that the U.S. and India have to negotiate for nuclear supply. There are actually other pieces of law and legislation that companies think are important to them in an economic sense that we'll have to see how those affect the ultimate trade. But at least those four big pieces have to go through before it's come together in a puzzle that says it's okay for the world and India to cooperate on civilian nuclear matters.

So we're proceeding on all those things. We've exchanged texts on a bilateral agreement. India sent somebody to the IAEA to start talking about the safeguards agreement. We've briefed the Nuclear Suppliers Group and we'll keep working with them. So we have all these pieces moving forward. When they can all come together, I don't know. It may take at least months, maybe a year at the best. But we'll get it done. It's a matter of making all those pieces come together properly....

Thank you.

The U.S.-India Civilian Nuclear Cooperation Agreement

15

Secretary **Condoleezza Rice**

April 5, 2006

Secretary Rice: Thank you very much, Senator Lugar, Mr. Chairman, members of the Committee. Thank you very much for this opportunity to come and discuss with you this indeed path-breaking U.S.-India civil nuclear cooperation agreement and it obviously deserves the support of the U.S. Senate, but we also understand that it deserves the thorough review of the Senate before giving that support. So that is why I'm here and I want to note that we are prepared to continue our discussions and our briefings to the point that you feel that you have the information that you need to make this determination.

Let me note that I have longer—a fuller testimony that I would like to have entered into the record.

Chairman Lugar: It will be made part of the record, in full.

Secretary Rice: Thank you very much. India's society is open and free. It is transparent and stable. It is multiethnic. It is a multi-religious democracy that is characterized by individual freedom and the rule of law. It is a country with which we share common values. India will soon be the world's most populous nation and America's exports to India have doubled in only the past four years. And of course, India is a rising global power that we believe can be a pillar of stability in a rapidly changing Asia. In other words, in short, India is a natural partner for the United States.

But for too long during the past half-century, during the Cold War in particular, because of both domestic policies and foreign policies, India and the United States were estranged. And one element of this estrangement was India's complete disregard—India's complete isolation from the policies that the

United States was concerned about concerning proliferation of weapons of mass destruction. Now, as a result of India's decision to have a nuclear program, to test nuclear weapons, to build a nuclear program, as did Pakistan, India's adversary in that region, we adopted non-proliferation policies to try and constrain and change Indian behavior.

But I think that it is entirely clear now that those past non-proliferation policies did not achieve their goals. In fact, they had no effect on India's development of nuclear weapons. They didn't prevent India and Pakistan from testing nuclear weapons in 1998. They contributed little to lessening regional tensions, which brought India and Pakistan repeatedly to the brink of war. And all of this simply resulted in a more isolated India, especially isolated from the standards and practices of the nuclear non-proliferation establishment that had been developing and maturing over the last decades.

Now, let us consider the future that we could have instead. The initiative that we are putting before you and asking for legislation to amend the Atomic Energy Act of 1954 will advance international security, enhance energy security, further environmental protection, and increase business opportunities for both our countries. All of these benefits must be viewed in this larger context, of course, of how the initiative itself elevates the U.S.-India relationship to the new strategic level that we desire.

The initiative, first and foremost, will deepen that strategic partnership. The United States and India are laying the foundation for cooperation on major issues in the region and beyond, building on and building up our broader relationship between our peoples and governments. I was just with President Bush in India and I can tell you that the discussion was broad and multifaceted. It was a discussion not just between governments, but between peoples, discussions about how to improve agriculture in India, much as we helped to spur the Green Revolution in India of the '60s.

We talked about the ability for India to access the new technologies to increase its agricultural production. There were discussions about Indian education and the desire for all of India's people to be able to access the new knowledge-based economy that is growing so rapidly in India. And of course, there were discussions between CEOs of Indian companies and American companies, showing that this is a broad relationship that is not just a government-to-government relationship, but one that is fundamentally affecting our societies.

Now, in order to fully realize the potential of this vision for India, we do have to deal with the long standing impediments associated with civil nuclear cooperation and we need to resolve them once and for all. We believe that this initiative will unlock the progress of our expanding relationship in other areas.

The initiative will clearly enhance energy security. India is a nation of over a billion people with an economy growing at approximately eight per cent each year. It has a massive and rapidly growing appetite for energy. It is now the world's sixth largest consumer of energy. Diversifying India's energy sector will help it to meet its ever increasing needs and more importantly, ease its reliance on hydrocarbons and unstable sources, like Iran. This is good for the United States.

Secondly, the initiative will benefit the environment. Nuclear energy is, after all, clean energy, and providing India with an environmentally friendly energy source like nuclear energy is an important goal. India's carbon emissions increased 61 per cent between 1990 and 2001; that number is surpassed only by China. This initiative will create opportunities for American jobs. Nuclear cooperation will provide a new market for American nuclear firms, as well as assist India's economic development. The initiative may add as many as three to 5,000 new direct jobs in the United States and about 10,000 to 15,000 indirect jobs in the United States, as the United States is able to engage in nuclear commerce and trade with India. By helping India's economy to grow, we would thus be helping our own.

Finally, this initiative does strengthen the international nuclear non-proliferation regime. I know that there has been a lot of concern about the Non-Proliferation Treaty and India's refusal to join and, indeed, the view that India should not join as a nuclear weapons state, a view that we continue to hold. I want to say to the Chairman and to the Committee that the United States values greatly the Non-Proliferation Treaty. It is one of the cornerstones of our non-proliferation policy, but of course there is a broader non-proliferation regime as well. And we believe that the continued isolation of our strategic partner from that regime is the wrong policy choice. The initiative is thus a strong net gain for non-proliferation in general.

I must just note that the custodian of the non-proliferation regime, Mohamed ElBaradei, has been from the very beginning a strong supporter of this initiative and he remains so. I should note also that Great Britain and France are strong supporters and Russia supports it as well. Both Prime Minister Blair and President Chirac have issued statements in that regard.

Now, I want to take just a moment to take head on, if you will, several criticisms that have made of the initiative. And let me associate myself with what the Chairman said, it is a path-breaking agreement. And of course, one always has to balance the various factors in deciding whether or not it is worth pursuing. We believe that the criticisms can be addressed and I will address them here.

Firstly, India would never accept a unilateral freeze or cap on its nuclear arsenal. We raised this with the Indians, but the Indians said that its plans and policies must take into account regional realities. No one can credibly assert that India would accept what would amount to an arms control agreement that did not include other key countries, like China and Pakistan.

Secondly, the initiative with India does not seek to renegotiate or amend the NPT. India is not and is not going to become a member of the NPT as a nuclear weapons state. We are simply seeking to address an untenable situation. India has never been party to the NPT and this agreement does not bring—but this agreement does bring India into the non-proliferation framework and thus strengthen the regime.

Thirdly, civil nuclear cooperation with India will not lead to an arms race in South Asia. Nothing we or any other potential international suppliers provide to India under this initiative will enhance its military capacity or add to its military stockpile. Moreover, the nuclear balance in the region is a function of the political and military situation in the region. We are far more likely to be able to influence those regional dynamics from a position of strong relations with India and indeed with Pakistan.

Fourthly, this initiative does not complicate our policies toward countries like North Korea and Iran. It is simply not credible to compare India to North Korea or to Iran. While Iran and North Korea are violating their IAEA obligations, India is making new obligations by bringing the IAEA into the Indian program and seeking peaceful international cooperation.

Iran and especially North Korea are, of course, closed non-democratic societies. India is a democracy. In fact, India is increasingly doing its part to support the international community's efforts to curb the dangerous nuclear ambitions of Iran.

In sum, the U.S.-India civil nuclear cooperation initiative is a strategic achievement. It's good for America, it's good for India and it's good for the international community. I know that there is a history that we are trying to overcome, but the time comes when you must deal with the realities and indeed overcome that history.

President Bush and I look forward to Congress as a full partner in this initiative. Your support for this legislation is crucial and we ask you to lend it. Together we can seize this tremendous opportunity to solidify a key partnership that will advance American interests, the ideals of peace and prosperity and liberty for which we stand.

Thank you, Mr. Chairman. I very much look forward to answering the questions of the distinguished members of the Committee.

Thank you.

U.S.-India Civil Nuclear Agreement

16

R. Nicholas Burns, Under Secretary of State for Political Affairs

March 22, 2006

Moderator: Good morning and welcome to this morning's briefing on the Indian Civil Nuclear Agreement. This morning we have with us Under Secretary of State Nicholas Burns. He'll give you a brief opening comment—I believe you've seen some materials on the agreement that we've put out front—and then be happy to take your questions.

Under Secretary Burns.

Under Secretary Burns: Good morning. It's a pleasure for me to be at the Foreign Press Center where I have not been in 10 years. It's changed a little bit and I'm happy to be back, happy to see all of you. I wanted just to say a few words about President Bush's initiative to seek congressional support for our civil nuclear agreement with the Indian Government. We have been briefing members of Congress for the last several weeks. Those briefings have gone very well. We've briefed members and staff. Next week, there'll be formal briefings of the relevant committees that have jurisdiction over the legislation and then the following week, Secretary Rice is going to be testifying before the Senate Foreign Relations Committee as well as the House International Relations Committee.

We're convinced this deal is positive for United States national security interest because it will help us first cement our strategic partnership with India, which is very important for our global interests. Secondly, it will provide a net gain for our hope to strengthen the proliferation regime because it will bring into the proliferation system for the first time in 30 years, one of the largest countries in the world and a country that hopes to have one of the largest civil, peaceful nuclear power industries in the future and that's India. And the calculation that we made, as we thought about this agreement over the last year is that we are far better off working with the Indians and having the IAEA place safeguards on India's nuclear—civil nuclear program than we are if India is isolated and fully sanctioned. And so we're seeking relief from U.S. law that currently prohibits American private investment and trade with India's civil nuclear sector. We're asking Congress to provide an India-only—and India-specific waiver to the Atomic Energy Act of 1954 and we're looking forward to the briefings of members, the formal briefings and of the hearings that will follow thereafter.

I'll be very happy to take any questions that you have on this particular arrangement. I think all of you are familiar with it, but I think it's best just to go right to questions.

Question: Mr. Burns, this is Sridhar Krishnaswami from The Press Trust of India. Has anybody had a chance to see yesterday there was a report in *The Washington Post* of respected senator—former Senator Sam Nunn, expressing serious reservations of this civil nuclear arrangement. I would want to know how you'd react to it, number one, and number two whether his comments would complicate Administration efforts on Capitol Hill?

Under Secretary Burns: Thank you very much. Senator—former Senator Nunn is a very respected individual and all of us, of course, appreciate the tremendous work that he has done for many, many years on the issue of proliferation. So we take his views very seriously and we have had a chance to talk to him, members of the Administration, and I know we'll continue to seek a dialogue with him.

I would say this, that the civil nuclear agreement with India is positive for our national interests because what we do believe, it will strengthen, not weaken the non-proliferation regime. The curious aspect of a current non-proliferation regime globally, is that some countries that are inside the regime, I'm thinking here of Iran and North Korea. They have not met their commitments to the NPT regime and, in fact, are cheating and have cheated on those commitments. And the anomaly is that some countries that are on the outside—and India is the most prominent of those—are adhering to the regulations of the non-proliferation regime, but they're not allowed in.

And so we had to answer, in our government, a fundamental question. In the real world in which we live, the world of relations among states, is it better for the United States and the rest of the world to keep India at arm's distance, to keep India out of the proliferation regime, to have no international safeguards to speak of on India's civil nuclear industry or is it better for us to bring them in, so that at least we capture three quarters of the Indian civil nuclear power system under international safeguards?

And we arrived at the conclusion, about a year ago, that far better off working with the Indians, because India is a country that is governed by the rule of law. India is a country that has not proliferated its nuclear material, unlike many other countries that are signatories to a non-proliferation regime. And therefore, India is a country that can be trusted and that the rest of the world wants to work with. We are assisted in this by Mohamed ElBaradei who is the defender and protector of the international non-proliferation regime. He made a public statement three weeks ago that he is fully in favor of the civil nuclear agreement between India and the United States because he thinks it's going to strengthen the non-proliferation regime. And Britain and France and Russia and Australia and many other countries have now come out to strongly support this agreement. So we think that, on balance, this is a net gain for proliferation and therefore we ought to go forward with it and we're seeking congressional legislation that would allow us to do that. And we have also sent Assistant Secretary Richard Boucher and Assistant Secretary Steve Rademacher to Vienna to address the Nuclear Suppliers Group tomorrow and they'll make a presentation to the Nuclear Suppliers Group that we think that that 45-nation body should agree by consensus to change its practice and to allow every country in the world to trade and invest in India's nuclear power sector.

Some of the criticisms of this agreement have been that—one is that this will somehow weaken our ability to work effectively internationally to place pressure on the Iranian Government to give up its nuclear weapons ambitions. Well, I am a person who's been working very intensely on that issue. I was in New York on Monday night for a meeting with the P-5 political directors and I can tell you, not a single country with which we deal has said, "We can't be tough on Iran because you Americans have this nuclear deal with India." It doesn't work that way. International politics doesn't work that way.

I think everybody recognizes a peaceful, democratic, law-abiding country that wants to come into the IAEA regime, India, versus a country that is autocratic, that has not told the truth about its nuclear ambitions, and that is actively trying to kick the IAEA out of its country, and that country is Iran. So it's a very clear and, frankly, stark juxtaposition of these two countries. And when I meet with the Russians and the Chinese and the Europeans and the Japanese and the Australians, none of these countries are saying, "Gee, because you've got this deal with India, we simply can't agree with you on Iran." That's not how the world works.

And I sense a great deal of commitment on the part of all the governments that I mentioned, particularly the governments of Russia and China, that we ought to deny Iran a nuclear weapons capability and all of us should work towards that end. All of us agree that Iran is in violation of its IAEA commitments and all of us believe that there should be a concerted action at the Security Council, hopefully in a matter of a couple of days of a presidential statement, to say that to the Iranians.

So the argument that somehow, by working with India on civil nuclear issues, we weaken the international effort against Iran, that argument, I think, carries no water, it has no weight, and it's not accurate. And so I think that, as we explain this deal to the Congress, we're going to be able to make a convincing case that this is in the interest of the United States of America.

Moderator: (Inaudible.)

Question: Chidanand Rajghatta from Times of India. Ambassador Burns—Secretary Burns, sorry—your colleague—you mentioned your colleague, Richard Boucher, has gone to

Vienna. Can you give us a sense of how the NSG countries stack up, for and against the deal? In particular, have you spoken to the Chinese and the Canadians and where do they stand on this deal?

Under Secretary Burns: I think it wouldn't be appropriate for me to characterize the views of other governments. One doesn't normally do that in diplomacy, so I won't do that this morning. But suffice it to say that when you have leading members of the NSG, the United States, Russia, Britain, France, Australia all speaking out in favor of this agreement, I think that's a fairly compelling group of countries. Now, we do have to reach a consensus in the Nuclear Suppliers Group. And my very strong sense is that what we're going to hear tomorrow is a lot of countries are going to wait and see if the United States Government is able to convince the U.S. Congress to pass the necessary legislation to allow this deal to go forward.

And once that happens, then I think sequentially, the Nuclear Suppliers Group will then want to take action on its own. And I'm confident that if the U.S. Government can convince the Congress to do what we're asking, I think that there'll be a very strong tide of support in the NSG in favor of this, but that's probably a few months away. This is a very complicated arrangement. Countries obviously have a right to look at it and be given the details and we'll be getting the necessary details when Ambassador Boucher and Assistant Secretary Rademacher brief the NSG countries.

Moderator: We're going to go do a question from our colleagues in New York, please.

Question: Under Secretary Burns, I'm with the CNBC TV 18. My name is Anirudh Bhattacharyya. I have a question about the statement recently from the Pakistan Foreign Ministry in which the office criticizes the India nuclear deal and it said that it altered the balance of power in South Asia and that will only encourage India to continue its weapons program without any constraint or inhibition. How do you react to those fears expressed by the Pakistan Foreign Ministry?

Under Secretary Burns: Well, let me say that we have a very good and strong relationship with the Pakistani Government as well as with Foreign Minister Kasuri personally. I met with him in Islamabad in January and, of course, Secretary Rice and I met with him on the margins of President Bush's visit to Islamabad.

And I think that, you know, what we have said to the Pakistani Government is that this arrangement between the United States and India is good for all of the countries of South Asia, including Pakistan, because India's nuclear program, civil nuclear program, which has been outside of international supervision, outside of international safeguards for 30 years, is now going to come into international safeguards and the IAEA is going to place safeguards on fully three-quarters of India's program. That ought to be, you would think, an attractive proposition to all the neighbors of India, including Pakistan.

I should also say that we've had a very full discussion with the Pakistani authorities. We've kept them informed in general on these negotiations for the better part of the year, so this didn't come as a surprise to the Pakistani Government. And our sense is that along with this deal should come a continued effort by the governments of Pakistan and India to obviously continue the good relations that they enjoy in a composite dialogue, that they should work on narrowing the differences they have on the range of issues between India and Pakistan, that they should continue to work to resolve the problem of Kashmir as they have been trying to do, and that the more positive developments in relations between those two countries should continue.

Restraining any sense of arms competition between India and Pakistan should be a very high priority for both governments. We've said that to both governments privately. We're very happy to say that publicly. And we're convinced that stability will be maintained in South Asia; we will not see the kind of arms race that some of the critics are now forecasting. We think that we'll continue to see an improvement in relations between India and Pakistan, and we're a friend to both and I think we're in a position to assess that as a reasonable prospect for the future.

Moderator: We'll go to Barry.

Question: This has been my question. I was going to suggest for decades the U.S. has maintained this exquisite balance between India and Pakistan. If there was any tipping, it was in Pakistan's direction rather than democratic India's. And I wondered how you—if this isn't an aberration and will it hurt relations with Pakistan? But I think basically you may have answered it by saying you're talking to the Pakistanis and explaining that it promotes stability.

Under Secretary Burns: Yes. Barry, thank you. And I think you're right to ask the question and, of course, you're drawing upon your experience of the last 30 years, as you remember from the 1970s, when this question was paramount in U.S. foreign policy. I think President Bush answered this question better than I could at his press conference in Islamabad just a couple of weeks ago when he said these two countries have different histories and they're different countries, and the United States wants to be, can be and shall be good friends and partners with both countries.

But as he and Secretary Rice have said very frequently, there's no need for us to have a hyphenated policy towards India-Pakistan. We ought to have a strong global partnership with India. We think, frankly, that one of the most important strategic initiatives of the United States in the last few years has been the opening to India, to see this incredible expansion of private sector ties between our two countries, the tremendous American private investment in India, particularly in the advanced technology sector, the tremendous expansion of trade which has benefited both of our countries.

We've also seen a real flourishing of ties between American citizens and Indian citizens. There are 85,000 Indians studying in the United States. It's the largest group of foreign students. We've seen a multiplicity of private sector ties: the Asian Society, our premier American non-governmental organization that looks at Asia—just opened a new center in Mumbai just last week. And so that private sector expansion has been coupled with the emergence of a key, now global partnership, between the Indian and American government, which we think is going to be critical for stability in Asia, in the Asian region, in South Asia as well as in the broader, the greater Middle East as we look to the future. So this relationship between India and the United States is singularly important for our society and for the future of American policy.

Now, I should also say that we have indicated now very clearly, and the President did so when he was in Pakistan, the centrality of the U.S.-Pakistani relationship. It's a different type of relationship than the U.S.-India relationship. Our relationship with Pakistan is grounded in our commitment to that country's security, to the fact that we are partners in our war against al-Qaida, of course there's an al-Qaida presence in part of Pakistan, and against the Taliban. It's our mutual commitment—Pakistan and the United States—to the safety and security of Afghanistan and of a more peaceful and stable border. And so we wish to see a growth in U.S.-Pakistani ties.

We are close to, I hope, resolving negotiations, finishing negotiations for a bilateral investment treaty. We brought to Islamabad some ideas about further American investment in Pakistan that we hope will lead to job creation, even in places like Balochistan and Waziristan where there's been high unemployment. So we have high hopes for the U.S.-Pakistan relationship. And there's no reason that we ought to somehow tie these two together so strictly that you limit the growth in either relationship. That's the way President Bush put it and that's how we see relations, Barry, between the United States and those two very important friends of ours in South Asia.

Question: How are you going to sell the deal to the Nuclear Suppliers Group? On the one hand, you'll tell them to loosen it in the case of India and then tighten it in the case of others? So there's a contradiction there.

Under Secretary Burns: There's no contradiction at all. There's no contradiction at all. I mean, it's not a contradiction to say to the Nuclear Suppliers Group or the U.S. Congress, "here's our friend India, a democratic country that plays by the rules. That has not diverted its nuclear technology, that wants to invite the IAEA to come in and inspect its nuclear facilities on a permanent basis so that the whole world will know what's going on inside the Indian nuclear—civil nuclear establishment."

And then here's another country, Iran, that lied to the IAEA for eighteen-and-a-half years about its secret nuclear research, that has just said to the IAEA, "We don't want the additional protocol," that has also said on January 4th that it's proceeding to enrichment research and development, which the Russian, Chinese, Indian, Egyptian, Sri Lankan, American, Japanese, Australian, and European governments have all said is a bridge too far, they crossed a line.

There is a dramatic difference between India and Iran, a dramatic difference, and all the world understands it. So when Ambassador Boucher and Ambassador Rademacher walk into the hall tomorrow and brief the Nuclear Suppliers Group, I think they're going to get a good reception. I don't think all the countries are ready to make a decision yet. They're going to want to see the details of this agreement and we'll give them the details. They're going to want to see what the U.S. Congress does and that's logical. And so this takes time, but we're confident that in the end, there's going to be—there will be a positive result.

Moderator: We'll go to VOA right there.

Question: You just said that you were talking to Pakistan before the deal happened, but the way Khurshid Kasuri has come out and President Musharraf later said, it shows that Pakistani leadership was not taken into that kind of confidence, that they could not prepare their people, given the bitter history between the two countries, to be prepared for this kind of a deal. Were the political implications of the deal taken into consideration?

Under Secretary Burns: I understand that Foreign Minister Kasuri has said he—and I think he informed us that he believes that he was misquoted in the *Financial Times* article last week. And we've had very good discussions with Minister Kasuri and Foreign Secretary Riaz Khan over the last several days. Pakistan is a friend and I think we have a good dialogue on this. We did keep the Pakistani Government fully informed of what we were doing over the last year in negotiating this civil nuclear agreement with India. I was in Islamabad in late January, six weeks before President Bush's visit to the region, and I did brief the Pakistani Government, as did our ambassador, Ambassador Crocker.

So there's not a problem between Pakistan and the United States. We're friends, we're partners, and I've had good conversations myself over the last 24 hours with senior officials in Islamabad and I think they fully understand the rationale of the United States. They may not agree with everything that we do, but that's normal in international politics. Even the best of friends sometimes disagree, but there's no sense of crisis and I think we'll move forward on a very good basis for the Pakistani Government.

Moderator: Let's go over here.

Question: Thank you very much, Mr. Secretary. Thank you for coming today.

Under Secretary Burns: Pleasure.

Question: My name is Ota with Japanese Kyodo News. I have a question. You say that some people—you characterize them as critics—they are concerned about the arms race based on this deal. So my question is congressional side is also putting the pressure on your side, put some condition, like a capping of fissile material productions, but if this deal doesn't go, maybe it doesn't seem to go anywhere, just reflecting the strong reaction from India's side.

So my recommendation—it's a cut-off treaty—

Under Secretary Burns: You're recommending to me—

Question: Cut-off treaty—

Under Secretary Burns:—on behalf of the Japanese media?

Question: Cut-off treaty, yes.

(Laughter.)

Under Secretary Burns: Okay, (inaudible).

Question: You have the administration's declared position: a cut-off treaty is unverifiable. So maybe because of this decision, (inaudible) discussion hasn't—you know, it looks like—don't go anywhere. So, I—you know, this position unverifiable, it's cut-off treaty. This option—is kind of feasible for your government to push away—push—you know, push to steer around, get some more weight out for final agreement with congressional side. Thank you very much, sir.

Under Secretary Burns: Thank you very much for your question and thank you for the recommendation. We look forward to your written proposal to us.

(Laughter.)

Under Secretary Burns: Thank you for raising this issue. The United States has said for a very long time that we are interested in a Fissile Material Cut-off Treaty. In fact, if you go back to the July 18th joint statement between Prime Minister Singh and President Bush here at the White House in Washington, both governments said that we will work together to support a fissile material cut-off treaty. And I think you'll see us in the near future push this idea forward. As you know, the United States and many of the other nuclear powers do have a moratorium on fissile material production and we encourage other countries to adopt the same practice. A treaty would be helpful. We've said that many times. The President said it in July. And I think you'll see us support that in the future.

Moderator: Let's go to *Al-Hayat*.

Question: Joyce Karam from *Al-Hayat* newspaper. My question is about the presidential statement that you're expecting from the United Nations. You announced a couple of weeks ago that it has been delayed. Why is this delay? And would it be a preliminary step before we see a potential resolution under Chapter 7 about Iran?

Under Secretary Burns: Thank you for your question. You know, we are working hard up in New York at the United Nations to achieve a presidential statement of the Security Council. This is important because we believe that the Security Council should speak with one voice to say the following, and here is the elements of a presidential statement: that the Iranian Government is in violation of its IAEA commitments; that all of the Security Council members, including all the permanent members, want to see Iran suspend its nuclear program and return to negotiations; and that would be to suspend the enrichment R&D that is currently underway this week at the Iranian nuclear facility at Natanz.

I was up in New York. I spent five and a half hours in discussions with the Russian and Chinese Governments, the European Governments, on Monday, and I think that there is sentiment that there should be a presidential statement. But you know, as you know, we're working multilaterally here and in any multilateral negotiation it's very complicated. I think we're united on the principles; we now need to find the right words to reflect that unity.

What I heard from the Chinese and Russian Governments the other night in the meeting were the following: that they agree with the United States and Europe that Iran should not be allowed to achieve a nuclear weapons capability. That's what they said in the meeting. They said that they agreed that Iran should come into compliance with its IAEA safeguards; it's not currently in compliance. And they also agreed that we are alarmed, all of us, by the speed at which Iran is now moving forward at that facility at Natanz on enrichment research and development.

And so if that's what is unifying the members of the permanent five countries and Germany and others, Japan and all the other members of the Council, then I think it's only a matter of time before we find the right words to memorialize that in a presidential statement. Things take time. These things take time in diplomacy. We're patient. We know that a clear, compelling statement of the Security Council is going to have an impact. And the impact will be that it sends a message, as the IAEA Board of Governors did on February 4th, that the Iranians are very much isolated in the world. When you have a collection of countries like Egypt and Ecuador and India and Brazil, Russia and China and Europe and Japan and Australia, all voting—and Canada—the same way with the same message, you would think the Iranians would have to stop and listen to that message. That would be the impact that a presidential statement has once it's agreed to.

Moderator: We have a follow-up here.

Question: Thanks a lot, sir. Dmitry Kirsanov of ITAR-TASS news agency of Russia. You said just a couple of minutes ago that you're hopeful that this presidential statement will be approved by the UN Security Council within several days. Foreign Minister Lavrov today indicated that Russia clearly would not support presidential statement in its current form because, as far as I understand, it gives Iran clear timeline, deadline within which it has to comply with the demands of the international community. Are you willing—is the United States Administration willing to soften its stance on that and, you know?

Under Secretary Burns: You know, we're in a negotiation. Negotiations take time and these are not easy negotiations because we're dealing with a complex issue involving nuclear weapons and so the stakes are very high. But what we have to do is stay focused on these negotiations and understand that in any multilateral institution like the UN it's going to require some patience, time, good faith effort and an inclination that all sides need to be flexible. I think that those ingredients can be there. And I don't know how long it's going to take. I don't know if it's going to be a couple of days or longer. It may be longer. But eventually I think that these countries are going to agree to a presidential statement because we essentially agreed and voted on a February 4th IAEA Board of Governors resolution that is quite similar in its substantive content to what is current under negotiations in New York at the United Nations.

Moderator: To Turkey, here.

Question: Umit Enginsoy with NTV Turkey. Mr. Secretary, in terms of non-UN Security Council nations, how would you like to see a major neighbor of Iran, Turkey, to behave on Iran's nuclear matter?

Under Secretary Burns: Well, I don't need to give public advice to an allied country like Turkey, but I think that Iran's neighbors all know that Iran is a problem in its own neighborhood. I mean, on the one hand, it's developing nuclear weapons against the wishes of the entire international community. I think the only countries that have voted to protect Iran on this issue are Cuba, Venezuela and Syria. So just consider those three countries but think of the rest of the world. The rest of the world clearly doesn't want that. Think of the fact that Iran has been central banker for the international terrorist organizations in the Middle East for 25 years now, and that's disturbing to Iran's neighbors. Think of the fact that particularly since President Ahmadinejad came into power in August, the Iranians have been flexing their muscles in their own neighbor and that's got a lot of their neighbors worried.

So I think the Iranians have, unfortunately for them, they've received so much attention later that they've become very isolated in the world and they're very much on the defensive, the Iranian Government. I think we'll have to keep them on the defensive so that we can move forward and make progress on all these issues internationally and maintain that unity that is clearly there. So I sense great unity in the international community as countries look at the problems that Iran causes in the international system.

Question: Mounzer Sleiman, with Al-Mustaqbal Al Arabi. The issue of strengthening the non-proliferation regime and placing IAEA at safeguards, there is a question out there why this agreement with India has not been preceded with a kind of agreement with IAEA on those safeguards, the issue of entering into agreement with a diminished role and the authority of the IAEA if it was not previously known that those safeguards are going to be implemented and agreed upon, especially from a country that did not agree or sign the NPT?

Going back to your argument also about the difference between India and Iran, for instance, now if Iran then get out of NPT, then it will be rewarded or will be offered some kind of incentives to go back to sign into the IAEA and will be given civilian as they claim they want to be—they want civilian. So the issue here—the argument, if the people are not signing will reward them—the people who they're signing and they may—

there is room to work with them and reinforce the safeguards and the supervision on the agreement—it's not there.

Under Secretary Burns: Well, let me just say this. I think we've gone over this ground many times in this briefing. The Director General of IAEA, Mohamed ElBaradei, has come out strongly in favor of the U.S.-India civil nuclear agreement. He said that he believes it will strengthen the international non-proliferation regime. Now no one is saying that about Iran, right now. And, you know, this deal with India is exceptional and it's unique to India because India is a unique place. It's a country that wants to commit to a system and live by the world's rules. It was not, you know, for historical reasons, allowed to come into that system in the 1970s, when it developed its nuclear program. It now wants to come in.

Iran, on the other hand, is a country that's trying to push everybody away and escape from the international system, so a difference could not be more stark. There is not a chance in the world that Iran would ever be offered a similar deal, as the one that the United States has just negotiated with India.

Another criticism that some people have made on the op-ed pages of our newspapers is, you know, if the United States and the NSG changed their international practice for India, what's to prevent this deal being offered to North Korea and Iran. I'll tell you what will prevent it, the international community. Forty-five nations of the Nuclear Suppliers Group all have to agree, come to a consensus, to change international rules. Now that's a logical proposition for India. If some country wanted to put Iran or North Korea and to nominate them for that treatment at the NSG, they wouldn't get any votes because no one would trust those countries—North Korea and Iran. That they would live by the rules of the international regime.

Moderator: Let's go in the back.

Question: Giampiero Gramaglia, ANSA. First of all, thanks for coming to brief us—

Under Secretary Burns: A pleasure.

Question:—and brief again as soon as you can.

Under Secretary Burns: As soon as I can, all right. It depends how you treat me. (Laughter.)

Question: I would like to go back to the Iran negotiation. You were referring to the need for patience and time. Is the American patience indefinite or there is a deadline for the American patience? And if you can, could you draw to us the similarities or the differences between the process going on now with Iran and the process we leave three years ago with Iraq?

Under Secretary Burns: Oh, I don't think there are any similarities at all between those two situations. I think that, you know, what you have now on the Iran question is a united international community. You have Russia and China and the United States working together. You have Brazil and India working with that group. You have Germany and France and Italy and Japan and Australia. It's a broad international group and we all say the same thing. We all agree on the message that should be given to Iran. And so I think this is a unique situation. And, frankly, you know, the United States now, for the last 12 months, has been supporting diplomatic efforts to resolve the problem. We supported the EU-3 negotiations between March 2005 and September 2005, until the time that Ahmadinejad walked out unilaterally of those negotiations. President Bush then said that he would support the Russian proposal to provide an offshore fuel arrangement to the Iranian Government. Well, Iran rejected that. And so we have consistently supported efforts by Russia and by the European countries on a reasonable basis to offer solutions to the Iranians, and the Iranians walk away from each of these offers.

And so you have to wonder what is motivating the Iranians to walk away, and we think it's because behind that guise, the guise of a peaceful nuclear program, is a nuclear weapons research program. It doesn't stand to reason that they'd be engaged in enrichment activities at Natanz for peaceful purposes, not at the rate that they're going it and not in the way that they're doing it—kicking out the IAEA inspectors so they can do their work in secret. What kind of message does that send to the rest of the world?

So what you've seen, you've seen a lot of countries band together, and that's been a very positive sign.

Moderator: We have time for one more quick one. Arshad.

Question: I am Arshad Mahmud and I am from Bangladesh. This is your sixth or seventh sort of briefing trying to explain—

Under Secretary Burns: Are you complaining? (Laughter.)

Question: No, no, no. (Laughter.)

Under Secretary Burns: Have you been to all of them?

Question: And you are scheduled to speak perhaps tomorrow again at the Council on Foreign Relations. Monday. Sorry. Anyway—

Under Secretary Burns: Are you coming to that?

Question: I hope so.

Under Secretary Burns: Good.

Question: My question is—

Under Secretary Burns: Have I convinced you yet? (Laughter.)

Question: No. (Laughter.)

Under Secretary Burns: You better come on Monday, then. (Laughter.)

Question: In this process, do you have any time to think about other countries in South Asia? Bangladesh, for example. (Laughter.)

Under Secretary Burns: Amid all these briefings on India?

Question: Yes, and Pakistan.

Under Secretary Burns: Yes, we do.

Question: And there are other countries that they have serious electricity problems, so and I'm just wondering, I have a question to you that Bangladesh is a signatory to NPT and do you have any time or have you given any thought to how to help on this civilian nuclear energy so that it can develop this power sector and develop the economy? Thank you.

Under Secretary Burns: Thank you for your question. First let me say that countries that are signatories to the NPT, unlike

India, then of course have, as they live by the rules of the NPT, they have the interest of all countries in the world to cooperate on electricity production through the growth of civil nuclear power. That's not a problem. India is an exceptional country because it's outside the system and so we try to bring it inside the system.

But let me just say in the case of Bangladesh, I was in Dhaka in June and I've worked very, very intensely on our relationship to try to build it into a strong relationship. We've given great support to the government and congratulate the government on the recent initiatives to crack down on the violent groups within Bangladesh who the government believes are responsible for the spate of bombings and intimidation in Bangladesh over the last six months. And we congratulate the government and the Prime Minister on the very good work that has been done.

We are very interested and involved in efforts to try to further trade and investment ties with Bangladesh. And I think in South Asia in general, I hope you will agree with me that the United States has been much more active in the past year or so than we ever had before in trying to work both bilaterally and regionally on all the issues that you mentioned. We've been a good friend to Bangladesh.

I was in Sri Lanka in January. We are a part of the group, along with Japan and the European Union, trying to support the negotiations to prevent a civil war in Sri Lanka between the government and the Tamil Tigers. We've been very actively involved in that and we'll continue to be.

We have been very actively involved in trying to give good advice to the Government of Nepal, and that would be to restore multiparty democracy as it continues to try to prevent a destabilization of the country by the Maoist rebels.

I think you've seen in the attention we've given to Pakistan as well as to India, you have an American Government now more actively involved in the affairs of South Asia than at any time since the era of decolonization began 60 years ago. That's because we have made a conscious decision that South Asia is critical to our long-term interests and that we want to build up these relations. Secretary Rice has led that effort for the United States Government. It is a conscious, deliberate effort.

So I can assure you, in between the briefings that we give to the press and the Congress on the India nuclear program, we have lots of people, including myself and Ambassador Boucher, focusing and thinking about South Asia, including your country.

I can take one more question.

Moderator: Let's go to Al-Ahram.

Question: Secretary Burns

Moderator: Here, please.

Question: —about the deadline of the American time limit. You forgot the first part of the question.

Under Secretary Burns: The line?

Question: Deadline.

Under Secretary Burns: Okay, deadline on—

Question: The deadline on American—

Under Secretary Burns: Oh, I'm sorry. I apologize. I was just so interested in your second question I forgot about your first question. (Laughter.)

Obviously we want to see a quick resolution of the problem concerning Iran's nuclear weapons ambitions. We also believe it's important to work diplomatically and to work effectively with Russia and China and the European countries and India and Brazil, and we'll do that with Japan—and we'll do that. So it's impossible to answer your question. I don't want to put a time limit on it. But I will say we're working with great urgency.

Question: Secretary Burns, Hoda Tawfik, Al-Ahram Egypt. Let me ask you, does this apply to countries in the Middle East with the United States seems—use the same—like the deal—similar deal with India to help other countries like Egypt to have peaceful nuclear programs?

Under Secretary Burns: Well, you know, the difference here is that the great majority of countries in the Middle East and your region are signatories to the non-proliferation regime. So therefore, you already have the ability to work with private

American companies to build nuclear power plants and to receive peaceful civil nuclear technology if you're a member of the NPT.

The case of India is India has not been allowed to be a member of the NPT. It's been kept outside the system. India is soon to be the largest country in the world by population. It is one of the greatest democracies of the world. It is a country that has always stood up for peaceful resolutions of disputes. It's a country that has not been aggressive towards its neighbors, but has been seeking to resolve problems with its neighbors. So it's an ironic situation and certainly, an anomalous situation when a great country like India is forced to stand outside of the system and we're just trying to bring India in.

Think what that means for a minute. India is accepting international oversight, accepting international inspections. Who can argue with that? Who wouldn't want to see the largest country in the world, the largest democracy in the world come into the international system and willingly submit itself to inspections? We think that's a net gain, a strong net gain for the international proliferation system and that's why we have proposed this agreement between our two countries.

Moderator: Thank you very much.

Under Secretary Burns: Thank you.

Ongoing Efforts to Implement the U.S.-India Civil Nuclear Agreement

17

R. Nicholas Burns, Under Secretary of State for Political Affairs

March 16, 2006

Mr. Ereli: Hello, everybody. Our first briefing today is going to be with Under Secretary of State for Political Affairs Nicholas Burns, who's here to talk—give you all an update on U.S.-Indian civilian nuclear cooperation. He'll start with some comments and take your questions.

Under Secretary Burns: Good morning. We're very pleased that on Capitol Hill today Senator Lugar on the Senate side and Chairman Hyde and Congressman Lantos on the House side will introduce legislation designed to grant exceptions for India to U.S. law that would permit the Administration to go forward and fulfill the terms of the civilian nuclear agreement that President Bush agreed to—with Indian Prime Minister Singh. We hope that this debate in the Congress will proceed swiftly. Secretary Rice was up on Capitol Hill last week. President Bush met with congressional leaders last week to discuss our hopes for congressional agreement on the India legislation. I have spent the better part of this week talking to members of the Senate and House about this.

We think this is a very important agreement for the future of U.S.-Indian relations and also the future of our country. Because if the Congress will agree to grant these India-specific exceptions to U.S. law and should the Nuclear Suppliers Group then agree to change international practice, we will be able to bring India into the mainstream of a non-proliferation regime and we believe this will be a strong net gain for non-proliferation, for our hopes and beliefs in non-proliferation. And all of you know,

I think, the terms of this agreement so I won't review them in detail except to say this, that India has agreed that roughly three-quarters of its nuclear system we've put under safeguards, India has agreed that all future civilian reactors, whether they're thermal reactors or breeder reactors, shall be placed under international safeguards. India has agreed that all of these safeguards shall be permanent. So once a nuclear plant is put under IAEA safeguards, it will be in perpetuity.

India has also agreed to align itself with the other international regimes concerning proliferation: The Australia Group, the Wassenaar Arrangement. India has agreed to maintain a moratorium on nuclear testing. India has also said that it will try—in fact, it was announced this week that it will tighten up its own restrictions on the export of any technology associated with this industry. And in fact India has an excellent record over 30 years of not diverting its nuclear technology.

So we're convinced this is a good deal, both for India and for the United States. We've also been in touch with a lot of countries around the world, particularly those that are members of the Nuclear Suppliers Group. We've been very pleased that Dr. ElBaradei, who in essence is the protector and defender of a non-proliferation system, he has spoken out positively, in writing, on behalf of this arrangement and that the French and British and Russian Governments have also supported it.

We do think that this deal can go forward—should go forward in the next several months. I know that there will be hearings on Capitol Hill and the Administration will be very happy to testify in those hearings. There'll be a series of briefings. I think for those of you from India who are here to report this, you should expect that this is going to be a somewhat lengthy process. It's likely to take several months, because that's the way the American process works as the Legislative branch reports—excuse me, the Executive branch reports to the Legislative branch and seeks congressional approval. But we are encouraged by the number of members of the Senate and the House who have spoken out publicly in favor of this agreement. And I think you'll see as the weeks go along, there'll be a number of co-sponsors in the Senate and House side to the legislation that is being introduced on Capitol Hill this afternoon.

There have been a number of objections made by members of the American public, the non-proliferation community, to this agreement and I'd be happy to talk to you about them. But we're confident that the Administration can answer the critics and respond to those objections. We certainly don't believe that in asking the international community to essentially treat India as an exceptional case, we don't believe that that is going to have a negative impact at all on other issues. For instance on the case of Iran, you have seen that the issue of Iran's pursuit of a nuclear weapons capability is now in New York at the United Nations.

And there'll be some important discussions early next week in New York, among the members of the Perm-5 and the German Government and others, about how we move forward with a presidential statement. And the whole world is focused on the Iranian nuclear question. Not a single country has come to us to say—not a single one—that this India nuclear deal has had any kind of impact on their thinking on how to deal with Iran, because we look at those two countries and we see a peaceful democratic India that is inviting the International Atomic Energy Agency to come into India and to place safeguards on the majority of its nuclear facilities. We see in Iran that it is essentially saying to the IAEA, get out of our country. Give us relief from the Additional Protocol. Give us relief from the inspection regime. So one country inviting the IAEA in, the other country trying to kick it out and that's quite a stark juxtaposition of views.

We also think it's very important to recognize that the only possible country that could achieve the kind of agreement that we'd like to see in the NSG would be India because other countries have proliferation problems. Countries like Iran and North Korea have so clearly violated their commitments that they wouldn't ever stand a chance of receiving exceptional treatment at the Nuclear Suppliers Group. So does India create a precedent that would somehow dilute the proliferation regime? Clearly not. In fact, I think a lot of countries around the world with which we have spoken believe that if India can come into the system, if the safeguards can be put into place, if India can meet these commitments to the international community which we think it can, it's going to strengthen that regime, not weaken it. So we're confident that this is a deal that is good for our country, as well as India, as well as a non-proliferation regime. And with that, I'll be happy to take any questions.

Question: Is the U.S. willing or agreeable to talking to Iran about its nuclear program—the senior negotiator (inaudible) talks and is that something that the U.S. will pick up on?

Under Secretary Burns: Well—

Question: Direct talks?

Under Secretary Burns: Yeah, we've taken note of the statements made this morning by Mr. Larijani. There have been earlier Iranian statements. You know, the problem here, Barry, is not the absence of discussions between the United States and Iran. The problem is what Iran is doing in its foreign policy. We see an Iranian Government, particularly since Ahmadinejad came to power in August, that seems bound and determined to create a nuclear weapons capability. Why else would they be undertaking the actions they have at the plant Natanz on enrichment research and development?

We see an Iranian Government that continues the 25-year Iranian preoccupation with supporting the major terrorist groups in the Middle East which have directed their fire at the United States, at American citizens, at Lebanon, at the Palestinians and at Israel. And we see a government that has unleashed, if you will, a much more aggressive foreign policy in its own region which I think has many countries in that region quite concerned.

So the problem here is not the absence of discussions between the Iranian Government and the American Government. The problem is and has been, for quite a long time, the actions of the Iranian Government.

Question: But there's opportunity to talk. I mean, you haven't responded to that. Why limit any discussion with them to their meddling in Iraq? Why not talk to them about their nuclear program if it's that awesome problem you've just outlined? Why—what harm would it be in talking to them?

Under Secretary Burns: Barry, we have made the calculation, particularly since the Ahmadinejad government came into being a couple of months ago, that it is better to try to isolate the Iranian Government. And so, you have seen and—what we've tried to do on the nuclear issue, for instance, the construction of this coalition of countries that voted against Iran on February 4th at the IAEA, Russia and China and Brazil and India, the United States, the Asian countries, the European countries. We believe that that has the attention of the Iranian Government. You see now Iranian envoys going to all sorts of capitals, throwing up into the air all sorts of ideas about how this problem can be resolved. But the Iranians haven't answered the central question that was raised on February 4th at the IAEA, and that is, will they be willing to suspend their nuclear activities at Natanz, to roll back the nuclear steps that they've taken since January and even before that and will they be willing to return to negotiations.

Why can't the Iranians accept the proposal made by the Russian Government many months ago for an offshore fuel arrangement? So this is where the international debate is and it's now in New York and that's a very serious forum. It's a more political forum than the technical nature of the discussions at the IAEA in Vienna.

And we're concentrating our attention on that multilateral forum, convinced that if the coalition of countries that is together in New York can send a united message to Iran that it has to roll back its nuclear activities and return to negotiations, that's the best way to deal with Iran. And so we choose that course. (Inaudible) trying to isolate, shine a spotlight on the Iranians and to ask the Iranians to respond to the clear role of all these countries around the world that spoke with one voice a month ago and continue to insist on the same behavior by the Iranian Government.

Question: Follow up, Nick?

Under Secretary Burns: Carol.

Question: How do you read the timing of the—

Under Secretary Burns: I just wanted to call on my friend Carol Giacomo—

Question: I'm sorry.

Under Secretary Burns:—who is seating here.

Question: I wanted to talk about India so—

Under Secretary Burns: Okay. Why don't we stay in Iran and then we'll go back to India.

Question: How do you read the timing of the Iranian acceptance to this offer, I believe Ambassador Khalilzad six months ago, said they're willing to talk about Iraq. Do you see it as linked to what's happening in New York? And secondly, what do you expect to come out of these talks if they happen on the Iraq issue?

Under Secretary Burns: Well, two separate questions. And the first question, as you know, I think Secretary Rice and other U.S. officials have said before that Ambassador Khalilzad had been authorized to undertake these discussions. However, these discussions have not taken place.

On your second question, which is what's happening in New York, we're hopeful that there will be an agreement on a presidential statement. Now these things take time in a multilateral organization like the United Nations. That was your question, right?

Question: (Inaudible).

Under Secretary Burns: And we're hopeful that presidential statement can be put together and that the Iranians can then take note of that and hopefully adjust their behavior.

Question: I was interested in your interpretation of why the Iranians picked today to say we're willing to talk to the United States about Iraq?

Under Secretary Burns: I have no idea why the Iranians chose today. But I would just say they've made similar statements for many months now.

Question: Mr. Burns, my name is (inaudible). I represent the *Daily Jang* in Pakistan. You made a contrast between India and Iran that one country has invited International Atomic Energy Agency to inspect and the other country has kicked them out and that is fine, as far as the current government goes. But let me go back—for eight years, the Khatami Government which was recognized as a reformist government by the United States and which had invited IAEA and had allowed them not only to inspect the facilities, but to put their seals on the Iranian nuclear facilities. Can you cite maybe two or three or even one encouraging economic concession that the U.S. Government made to that previous government to show support for its willingness to open its government facilities and to be reformist and to take on the fundamentalists?

Under Secretary Burns: Well, the —

Question: What did the United States do to encourage that government and to prevent people like Ahmadinejad to come into power?

Under Secretary Burns: The American Government is not in the habit of making concessions to countries that direct and fund terrorist groups that strike at American citizens and at friends of the United States, like Israel or Lebanon or moderate Palestinians. We're not in the habit of doing that and so we haven't done that. And the previous Iranian Government continued the long Iranian tradition of funding and directing terrorist groups in the Middle East. We believe a previous Iranian Government also had as a strategic long-term objective the creation of a nuclear weapons capability. And so you have to choose in diplomacy your tactics. And the tactics of the United States and most other countries have been to tell the Iranians that that kind of behavior is unacceptable. And so we've done that.

Now with the appearance of the Ahmadinejad Government, if you will, the problem has worsened. It's been exacerbated by the statements of that government concerning Israel, by the aggressive foreign policy towards some of its other neighbors and by now the provocative and quite dangerous steps that they've taken since January to cross the international redlines at their plant at Natanz to begin research and—centrifuge research and development. So we just have to judge countries by what they do, not just by what they say. And the previous Iranian government was engaged in all of these nefarious activities.

Now we did see on March 11, 2005, a public statement by Secretary Rice a year ago, that the United States would support the EU-3 negotiations with Iran. And that to show our interest in those negotiations, although we didn't participate in them, we would agree to the sale of spare parts by United States—American firms to Iran's aging fleet of airliners. And we would not object to Iran's application to begin the application to join the World Trade Organization. So, you know, we put those two forward but what happened? We saw the Iranian Government unilaterally end its negotiations with the EU-3. We saw them reject the Russian proposal and we saw them cross the international redlines on centrifuge research and development. So for all those discussions the Iranians have spurned all the offers. They've gone on unilaterally and it's in a direction that the entire international community has condemned.

And so we think the policy of the United States, which is to be tough-minded and expect that Iran will meet its commitments and to try to align ourselves with other countries in a large coalition to send one message, we think that policy is succeeding and we hope the Iranians hear this message.

Question: Just one follow-up. Mr. Burns, one follow-up.

Question: How is the policy succeeding?

Under Secretary Burns: Oh, I think if you look back, Carol, a year ago—

Question: The Iranians are continuing their program.

Under Secretary Burns: A year ago, there was a very limited international discussion about Iran's nuclear program. It had to do with three EU countries—been going on for some time with Iran. If you look at the last 12 months, we have been able to put together a much larger international coalition of countries. It is not insignificant that Russia and China and India and the United States are in one place on this issue. We were not in one place a year ago. And we're betting that Iran is not going to want to isolate itself. It's not a country like North Korea, which seems to thrive on isolation. It's a country that needs investment. It needs the kind of diplomatic ties that have been produced between Iran and some countries.

And I think what's at stake is the normalcy of those relations with part of the rest of the world should Iran not respond to this united that has been put forward.

Question: I don't think that the diplomacy has certainly been more deft until you got to the UN and now the Russians are throwing up huge roadblocks to moving forward on something that arguably, given what's gone before in the IAEA, should have been a rather *pro forma* presidential statement. But the facts on the ground remain the same, and that is, Iran's program moves inexorably forward if all the opinions of world leaders are to be believed.

Under Secretary Burns: I think it's going to be difficult for the Iranian nuclear program to move inexorably forward as you say, if they have to do it in isolation and if there is opposition from some of the friends of Iran, the countries that have dealt with Iran economically. The Russians, of course, have been engaged in the construction of a nuclear power plant in Bushehr for a number of years. All of that's going to be at stake if the Iranians don't respond to the message that they have to be hearing these days. So you know, we have to stay focused on a patient, determined, diplomatic course and that's what we're on.

You know, in New York, things do take time at the United Nations, but we're confident that we'll get to a presidential statement and confident that Iran's going to feel that pressure from the United Nations Security Council.

Question: A question about India.

Under Secretary Burns: Yes.

Question: Sorry.

Under Secretary Burns: Ladies first. (Laughter.)

Question: Thank you. Well, you're obviously having to do a lot of convincing about this nuclear deal with the Congress, also the think tanks. Now with this news of Russia wanting to sell fuel to India and saying that it's not in violation of any law—not in violation of the NSG, do you think future hearings and briefings—this is going to make it more difficult for you? What have been the real roadblocks here? When you go out and make your pitch, when you give your explanation for wanting to do this exclusive deal with India, what is it that they come back and tell you? You have spoken so many times. What are the doubts that still remain?

Under Secretary Burns: Well, there's—I now have been back from India for two weeks and I've had—gosh, I've met a countless number of senators and congressmen. This is a very complex agreement and it's quite esoteric in some respects. And so I think the Congress has a right to expect full briefings by the Administration, which we are now in the course of under—of doing, further testimony so that we can spell out, in some detail, exactly what has been agreed to and what the ramifications of this might be for the non-proliferation regime and for our relations with other countries.

And as President Bush said the day this deal was made in New Delhi, it is a difficult set of negotiations and what we're essentially doing here is establishing a new course, a new way of trying to strengthen the non-proliferation regime. So, we expect a vigorous debate on Capitol Hill because there's a lot at stake. We're confident that what we'll put forward is right for the United States, is right for our non-proliferation concerns, and we've been gratified that there have—that a considerable number of senators and representatives have spoken out publicly in favor of the agreement.

Very few members of Congress have spoken out against the agreement. There's a large group of members of Congress, a large group, who I think are waiting to hear the briefings, to hear the testimony, to be able to ask the questions that they have a legitimate right to ask. And so I think the debate—you know, hasn't been fully joined on Capitol Hill, but will be fully joined in a couple of weeks as the House International Relations

Committee and the Senate Foreign Relations Committee schedule the briefings and hearings that they tell us they want to have at the end of March and the beginning of April.

And I think it's quite legitimate for members of Congress to expect that we will have to present these views in some detail before they pronounce themselves and we expected that, given the nature of this agreement and given the fact that it is a departure from 30 years of orthodox thinking, conventional thinking in our own country about how best to achieve proliferation. But the argument we're making is this is not just good for the strategic relationship between India and the United States. It's not just good for jobs in the United States, and it will produce jobs in the United States.

It's good because we had a non-proliferation regime that wasn't working well, because the largest country in the world—in a few years' time when India overtakes China in population—was outside the system. And yet, that country had not diverted its nuclear material, wanted to come into the system partially, at least in civilian aspects, and wanted the kind of open trade that had been denied it for 30 years. We think it is an obvious gain to bring that country into the international system. Now, it takes a change in U.S. law, which we're asking the Congress to consider, and a change in Nuclear Suppliers Group practices.

So, I think you should expect—we expect it's going to be several months of debate, both in the United States and in the NSG, before we can complete this process. We expected that. So, my initial sense of two weeks of talk on Capitol Hill is that we've made our presentation, at least the first round of it, we're encouraged by the support that we have, but we also know that there's a great number of members of Congress who need to have further discussions and further testimony and that's ahead of us.

Question: But how confident are you that it will eventually go through with (inaudible)?

Under Secretary Burns: Well, that's up to the Congress to decide. We have a separation of powers in the United States and I wouldn't want to predict what Congress is going to do, but we're very hopeful that Congress will support the deal. We're asking members to support it. We think we're putting a good case before the Congress, but I want to be respectful of the prerogatives of the senior members of Congress who run these committees and I would leave—you know, the decision is to them, but we're hopeful and we think this is a good deal for our country.

Question: If I could follow on that, Nick. Neither chairman in the House nor the Senate has yet spoken out in favor of this and some Republicans have told me that Chairman Hyde, in particular, had some very serious concerns about it. Is that a fair assessment of things? Senator Lugar, clearly, from reading his statement, has taken a wait-and-see attitude. How hard were you working on them and how essential are they, particularly Senator Lugar's backing, to the process of moving forward?

Under Secretary Burns: You know, I don't think it would be appropriate for me to discuss our conversations with individual members, particularly the senior members. And I just think it wouldn't be—this is not the right place to do that.

I will say, however, that President Bush met with the congressional leadership last week and had a very good discussion with the leadership. Secretary Rice was able to have good meetings with the committee chairs last week. When she returns from Australia early next week, she intends to pick up where she left off and have a series of conversations on Capitol Hill next week. We are not discouraged by our contacts on Capitol Hill. We are encouraged by the numbers of senators and representatives who tell us, "You are on the right track. We like the agreement."

Now, a lot of them have technical questions or they want to see the full development of our argument and testimony, and that is to be expected and welcomed in our system. But what I'm trying to signal here is not discouragement. I think that we are in—you know, round one of a 15-round match and—because there's a lot that's ahead of us in terms of debate with the Congress and we want to be respectful of that process, but we're encouraged by the number of people on Capitol Hill who tell us, "Go ahead with this. This is a good idea and we'll support you."

Question: Nick, I have a follow-up to that particular question. You mentioned right at the outset that it will be Senator Lugar and Congressman Lantos who will be dropping the bill. Is there any significance to the fact that—

Under Secretary Burns: I think I said—just to be accurate, as I understand it, Senator Lugar on the Senate side, Chairman Hyde and Mr. Lantos on the House side will introduce the bill for debate.

Question: Okay. No, I thought—you hadn't mentioned the name Hyde, you said—

Under Secretary Burns: I did—I believe I did in my opening comments.

Joel: yes.

Question: When you're talking to the senators and congressmen, what are the most common concerns you're hearing?

Under Secretary Burns: Well, let me—that's an unbalanced question and I'll give you a balanced answer. We're hearing—

Question: (Inaudible)

Under Secretary Burns: Which is my prerogative—well, I'll answer your question—which is my prerogative. We're hearing a lot of support for the fact that we're trying to take a very difficult issue, how to have a functioning and effective non-proliferation system, and include in that this very large country that has a nuclear power industry and wants to expand the nuclear power industry, a lot of support for that and a lot of support for the design of the approach that we've made.

One of the issues, I think, that senators and representatives have been asking about is what happens in the future. Because the agreement announced in Delhi two weeks ago is a snapshot of the current situation: 14 to 22 power reactors to be put under safeguards; all future civilian reactors under safeguards, permanent safeguards.

Our assessment is this, that if Congress changes the legislation, approves this deal, if the NSG does so as well, India is going to embark on a massive expansion of its civil nuclear power sector and that the great majority of Indian investment in the nuclear industry will fall on the civilian side. The Indians tell us that eventually, they believe that 80 or 90 per cent of their nuclear system is going to be under safeguards, because the imperative in India is to increase power production, electrical power production through the growth of nuclear power plants.

And so some of the critics say this deal is going to lead to an expansion of India's nuclear weapons arsenal. We disagree with that fundamentally. Our assessment, based on one year of negotiations with the Indian Government, is that, of course, while they have a sovereign right to continue to modernize their nuclear weapons sector, and obviously, like any country, they will maintain and modernize it, we believe the great majority of the growth—not all of it, but the great majority is going to be on the civilian side.

Now, the Indian commitment to us in the separation plan, which I believe you probably all have a copy of, is that all future civilian thermal and breeder reactors will come under safeguards. So, as they add 1000-megawatt power plants, which we believe they will do in the near future, they will come under safeguards. And therefore, the percentage of increase, whether it's the number of reactors or megawattage under safeguards, is going to increase over time. And I think that's been an impressive argument, as I perceive it, from members of Congress to understand. And you'll note that the critics, when they write their op-ed pieces from the ivory towers or the think tanks, don't focus on that.

I think, Joel, to answer your question specifically, now that I've given you a balanced presentation, I think that—you know, members—as I said before, I don't want to be needlessly repetitive. This is a very complex agreement and it does break from the rep—the conventional wisdom of the past. So I think members are looking for testimony that will lay out this plan in some detail. They're going to want to ask questions. Some of them have suggestions that they've already made to us.

Now, we've said to members of Congress we do not wish to renegotiate this deal, because if you tried to open it up and renegotiate it, you probably wouldn't be able to put it back together again. But we have said to members, we would be—if you can get us ideas that do not require us to renegotiate the deal, but that might strengthen it by asking the United States or, for instance, to certify certain things that may happen in the future, that would be welcome. And we've already received such ideas.

And I think a lot of the—you asked—I think a lot of the questions coming from Congress are in that realm. And I think there is also a sense, you know, are the United States and India committed to a fissile material cut-off treaty? The answer is yes. We said that on July 18th when the Prime Minister was here; we've said it again in Delhi two weeks ago. Do we believe that it's possible to restrain an arms race in South Asia? And the answer to that is yes. The United States believes that India and Pakistan should continue with a very good composite dialogue that has taken place before their foreign secretaries, that both countries have an interest in minimizing any sense of competition. So we're trying to deal here with the questions that have been asked and somewhat criticisms that have been made. And we think we're responding effectively.

I don't know if you saw Secretary Rice's op-ed piece in *The Washington Post*. But I think she laid out there and she said that we sent that to every member of Congress. She sent a letter to every member of Congress. We gave factual detail in a package we sent to them two days ago. I think we're beginning to answer, one by one, all these questions that have been posed, whether it's on the Hill or in the press. And I think we're heading in the right direction in that respect.

Question: Can I follow-up on the non-proliferation—

Question: (Inaudible) he may put conditions on this legislation. Do you think that you can prevent conditions from being put on? I heard what you said about the President certifying certain things. A lot of lawmakers want to see the peaceful nuclear cooperation agreement before they tackle this legislation. How long will it take you to negotiate that agreement and are you willing to hold this legislation until that agreement is negotiated? And thirdly, you make and you repeat over and over again what a wonderful non-proliferation record India has. David Albright last week, as you may be aware, put out a report which calls into question, raises some serious questions about India's record. How do you respond to that?

Under Secretary Burns: Okay. Thank you, Carol. Pertaining to the—what we call the 123 Agreement, the bilateral civil nuclear agreement. We have gone through a year of negotiations with India on the really tough issues and we've worked them out. The bilateral agreement is a largely technical agreement that will not entail a tremendous amount of give and take between the two governments because we've resolved the issues. They will simply be reflected in the bilateral agreement. So we gave the Indian Government a draft copy of the text two days ago. And I think that that agreement should proceed expeditiously. It would surprise me if it took much time at all and what we've assured members of Congress is we're happy to share the text with them. We're happy to talk through the details of that agreement. But the bigger conceptual agreement is a separation plan that the 123 is largely technical. So I don't see those as a real problem.

Question: I'm just raising that because it's a concern of—

Under Secretary Burns: Understood. And I've heard the same request from members of Congress.

Question: How about—

Under Secretary Burns: On David Albright, let me just—on David Albright. I actually have not read through all of his briefings, so I don't want to be unfair to him and, you know, try to discuss it without being fully informed of everything he said and I'd be—I know we're happy to sit down with him and talk. It's interesting that, you know, a lot of countries around the world have a lot of experience with India in a nuclear realm. And of course, a lot of countries have taken a close look at India's record on non-proliferation. And the consensus that I hear, talking to most of the members of the Nuclear Suppliers Group, is that we all agree on one thing.

India, while it's been outside the NPT has conformed to a lot of the practices of the countries inside the NPT, which is another anomaly of India's current state. And all of us agree that India does have a good record in not proliferating its nuclear technology and nuclear materials. So people are free to make charges, whatever charges they want. That is the consensus opinion internationally. We have not seen anything that would indicate to us that there's any serious problem that would allow us to question the basic agreement we've made, which is that India is a country that when it makes commitments, follows up on those commitments and adheres to its international agreements. We believe that's the case with the Indian Government, that it's a trustworthy partner.

On the first question, again, we want to be respectful of the congressional process. So I don't want to answer—respond to what individual members may have said outside of the discussions we've had. This is a complex agreement. To reopen it, we're probably at risk of never being able to achieve it again and to reassemble it. So what we've said to members of Congress who have raised this with us is that we welcome all ideas. There may be ideas that do not require renegotiation, that may help to reinforce or strengthen this agreement. We're open to all of them. But we wish not to renegotiate.

Question: One of the problems that's always been an issue with India is expert controls. Are you satisfied that their export control law allows them—enables them to control exports of items controlled by the NSG and are they adhering to the guidelines of NSG unilaterally as they said they would? And also have they committed to join the Proliferation Security Initiative and, if not, why not?

Under Secretary Burns: Thank you very much. We believe that the passage in June by the Indian parliament of the weapons of mass destruction export control law was a significant step forward by the Indians. I think had they not done that, it probably would have made the July 18th agreement and the subsequent agreement of two weeks ago impossible to attain. Because it gave the Indians a foundation of compliance with international practice on export controls, so we were pleased by that. India is trying to align itself with all the practices of the Nuclear Suppliers Group.

And on your third question on the Proliferation Security Initiative, we're very hopeful that India will decide to join the Proliferation Security Initiative. There are a number of things that India has under discussion—as I said before, alignment with some of the other international regimes, Wassenaar and Australia Group. PSI is important. It's now a worldwide system that has been very helpful in the fight against proliferation and we think India should be part of it and it's India's decision whether or not to join, but we think it should and we're hopeful that it will.

Question: A follow-on on Joel's question (inaudible). Based on the conversations you and other Administration officials have had up on the Hill so far, in the broadest possible sense, would you say you're hearing more objections or just more technical questions, requests for information, desire for more detail?

Under Secretary Burns: To be very specific, we're hearing a lot of support and we're hearing a lot of questions. There are very few members of Congress who have told us, "We are opposed to this and we will vote against it." I think there's one member of Congress I've talked to who has said that, in the House of Representatives, and that's it. I think most members are—this is a very serious proposition. They want to look into it carefully.

What we did last week was to offer the House staff and the Senate staff, staff briefings. So, briefings by our negotiating team with the staff. That has now taken place. There have been two of them. There will be more of those to come. I think it's reasonable to expect that Under Secretary Joseph and I will go up and do further formal briefings. And then there will be testimony in the House and Senate and we're going to offer the highest-level Administration witnesses that we can.

Question: Could you comment a bit, please, on the deal between Russia and India, for Russia to supply uranium? I understand there's been some concerns by the State Department about this deal?

Under Secretary Burns: Well, you know, I would answer your question this way: India needs energy. For an economy growing at eight to nine percent a year, a billion people in the country, a rapidly expanding infrastructure, they need energy. So everyone understands that and in fact, the basis of our own agreement on civil nuclear technology is based on the need for energy.

We think the proper sequencing would be that if India needs nuclear fuel for its reactors at Tarapur, which I think—I believe is the question here. That the proper way to do this would be to have the U.S. Congress act and hopefully change our laws, have the NSG, more particularly, act and change NSG practices, and then countries—the United States, France, Russia—would be free to engage, at that point, in civil nuclear trade with India. And we think that that's the proper sequencing and we—I know that Adam Ereli and others have spoken this week and that reflects the views of our government.

Question: So if it goes ahead before they fulfill the agreement, you're opposed to it?

Under Secretary Burns: Well, I gave you the answer I wanted to give and that is that the proper sequencing would be the one that I laid out. And it's important that the international community have confidence that it's had a chance to voice its own opinion. Of course, before you go too far ahead, we've made that clear to both governments.

Question: Mr. Burns, I assume that you just said it falls through Congress, doesn't go through—where would it leave the U.S.-India relations?

Under Secretary Burns: I make it a practice—I used to stand up at another podium across the hall ten years ago—never to answer hypothetical questions. We are hopeful that the Congress—we are hopeful that the Congress will agree with the Administration and I don't want to engage in any kind of hypothetical answer that would take us off that.

Mr. Casey: I think we have time for just one or two more.

Question: I have a question on India. You've gone ahead with this deal. I mean, it kind of flaunts—

Under Secretary Burns: Carol, I guess you would have to ask both governments for their public rationale. I gave you an answer that I thought reflected the views in our own government and we've made those views known to both of the governments privately.

Question: Did either of them let you know in advance that they were doing it?

Under Secretary Burns: Yes, they did. Both of them did.

Question: And did you say—

Under Secretary Burns: I said essentially—we said essentially, in private, what I just said publicly.

Mr. Casey: This is the last question, Nick.

Question: In view of referring Iran to the Security Council and in view of the President Bush speech expected about reaffirming the pre-emptive war doctrine, do you expect that the problem with Iran is eventually going to be solved diplomatically or through use of force?

Under Secretary Burns: We are clearly attempting to send a very strong signal to the Iranian Government that it is isolated on this question of nuclear weapons and that the whole world is speaking with one voice and therefore, they ought to listen to that voice. And there's a process underway in the United Nations Security Council designed to shine a bright spotlight on Iran and have Iran pull back from its nuclear ambitions. We hope Iran will respond to that diplomatic course.

Thank you very much.

Secretary Condoleezza Rice: Our Opportunity with India

18

March 13, 2006

The week before last, President Bush concluded a historic agreement on civilian nuclear cooperation with India, a rising democratic power in a dynamic Asia. This agreement is a strategic achievement: It will strengthen international security. It will enhance energy security and environmental protection. It will foster economic and technological development. And it will help transform the partnership between the world's oldest and the world's largest democracy.

Firstly, our agreement with India will make our future more secure, by expanding the reach of the international non-proliferation regime. The International Atomic Energy Agency would gain access to India's civilian nuclear program that it currently does not have. Recognizing this, the IAEA's director general, Mohamed ElBaradei, has joined leaders in France and the United Kingdom to welcome our agreement. He called it "a milestone, timely for ongoing efforts to consolidate the non-proliferation regime, combat nuclear terrorism and strengthen nuclear safety."

Our agreement with India is unique because India is unique. India is a democracy, where citizens of many ethnicities and faiths cooperate in peace and freedom. India's civilian government functions transparently and accountably. It is fighting terrorism and extremism, and it has a 30-year record of responsible behavior on non-proliferation matters.

Aspiring proliferators such as North Korea or Iran may seek to draw connections between themselves and India, but their rhetoric rings hollow. Iran is a state sponsor of terrorism that has violated its own commitments and is defying the international community's efforts to contain its nuclear ambitions. North Korea, the least transparent country in the world, threatens its neighbors and proliferates weapons. There is simply no comparison between the Iranian or North Korean regimes and India.

The world has known for some time that India has nuclear weapons, but our agreement will not enhance its capacity to make more. Under the agreement, India will separate its civilian and military nuclear programs for the first time. It will place two-thirds of its existing reactors, and about 65 per cent of its generating power, under permanent safeguards, with international verification—again, for the first time ever. This same transparent oversight will also apply to all of India's future civilian reactors, both thermal and breeder. Our sale of nuclear material or technology would benefit only India's civilian reactors, which would also be eligible for international cooperation from the Nuclear Suppliers Group.

Secondly, our agreement is good for energy security. India, a nation of a billion people, has a massive appetite for energy to meet its growing development needs. Civilian nuclear energy will make it less reliant on unstable sources of oil and gas. Our agreement will allow India to contribute to and share in the advanced technology that is needed for the future development of nuclear energy. And because nuclear energy is cleaner than fossil fuels, our agreement will also benefit the environment. A threefold increase in Indian nuclear capacity by 2015 would reduce India's projected annual CO_2 emissions by more than 170 million tons, about the current total emissions of the Netherlands.

Thirdly, our agreement is good for American jobs, because it opens the door to civilian nuclear trade and cooperation between our nations. India plans to import eight nuclear reactors by 2012. If U.S. companies win just two of those reactor contracts, it will mean thousands of new jobs for American workers. We plan to expand our civilian nuclear partnership to research and development, drawing on India's technological expertise to promote a global renaissance in safe and clean nuclear power.

Finally, our civilian nuclear agreement is an essential step toward our goal of transforming America's partnership with India. For too long during the past century, differences over domestic policies and international purposes kept India and the United States estranged. But with the end of the Cold War, the rise of the global economy and changing demographics in both of our countries, new opportunities have arisen for a partnership between our two great democracies. As President Bush said in New Delhi this month, "India in the 21st century is a natural partner of the United States because we are brothers in the cause of human liberty."

Under the president's leadership, we are beginning to realize the full promise of our relationship with India, in fields as diverse as agriculture and health, commerce and defense, science and technology, and education and exchange. Over 65,000 Americans live in India, attracted by its growing economy and the richness of its culture. There are more than 2 million people of Indian origin in the United States, many of whom are U.S. citizens. More Indians study in our universities than students from any other nation. Our civilian nuclear agreement is a critical contribution to the stronger, more enduring partnership that we are building.

We are consulting extensively with Congress as we seek to amend the laws needed to implement the agreement. This is an opportunity that should not be missed. Looking back decades from now, we will recognize this moment as the time when America invested the strategic capital needed to recast its relationship with India. As the nations of Asia continue their dramatic rise in a rapidly changing region, a thriving, democratic India will be a pillar of Asia's progress, shaping its development for decades. This is a future that America wants to share with India, and there is not a moment to lose.

U.S.-India Civil Nuclear Cooperation Initiative

19

March 9, 2006

On March 2, 2006, President Bush and Prime Minister Singh announced in New Delhi that the United States and India have reached a historic agreement on civil nuclear cooperation. This initiative reflects the profound transformation in United States-India relations, a partnership that will promote democracy, stability, prosperity, and peace in the region and globally.

Under India's civil military separation plan, which forms part of the U.S.-India civil nuclear cooperation initiative, India has agreed to:

- Place a majority of its existing power reactors and those under construction (14 of 22) under IAEA safeguards, and to place other associated upstream and downstream facilities that support those reactors under safeguards;
- Place all future civilian thermal power and civilian breeder reactors under safeguards;
- Negotiate a safeguards agreement that would place all Indian civilian nuclear facilities under safeguards in perpetuity;
- Permanently shut down the CIRUS reactor in 2010, shift the fuel core of the Apsara reactor purchased from France outside the Bhabha Atomic Research Center and place it under safeguards in 2010; and
- Identify and declare nine other research facilities as civilian.

In addition, under the initiative, India has pledged to:

- Negotiate and sign an Additional Protocol with the IAEA;

- Implement through appropriate rules and regulations India's recent passage of the Weapons of Mass Destruction Act of May 2005, creating a robust national export control system;
- Refrain from transfers of enrichment and reprocessing technologies to states that do not already possess them and support efforts to limit their spread;
- Work with the United States to conclude a multilateral Fissile Material Cut-off Treaty;
- Continue its unilateral moratorium on nuclear testing; and
- Adhere to the Missile Technology Control Regime (MTCR) and the Nuclear Suppliers Group (NSG) guidelines.

This agreement has several specific and important benefits.

Firstly, it deepens the U.S.-India strategic relationship,whose broadening scope will help ensure stability, prosperity, and peace in Asia and worldwide.

Secondly, the initiative will open significant business opportunities for American firms, as they will increasingly help meet India's demand for civilian nuclear technology, fuel, and support services. This translates into new jobs, incomes and markets for the United States.

Thirdly, it will help meet India's surging energy requirements in an environmentally friendly manner. The initiative enables India to rely increasingly on nuclear technology which is "clean" in comparison to other technologies, and will decrease India's dependence on foreign oil and gas imports, such as those from Iran.

Finally, this initiative brings India into the global nuclear non-proliferation mainstream. For the first time, India has committed to take the significant steps described above that will end its 30 year isolation from the global regime and will increase the transparency of its civilian nuclear program, improve the safety and the effectiveness of that program, and provide oversight—again for the first time—over a large majority of

Indian civilian nuclear reactors and the associated upstream and downstream facilities that support these reactors.

For its part, the United States is committed to working with the U.S. Congress to amend relevant domestic law to allow full peaceful nuclear cooperation with India, and to seeking agreement within the Nuclear Suppliers Group to accommodate this cooperation. The United States will also negotiate a bilateral agreement on peaceful nuclear cooperation with India and seek to assure the reliable supply of nuclear fuel to India through multiple avenues and instruments.

This initiative represents the culmination of many months of diplomacy on both sides and symbolizes the broader meaning of the President's visit to India, which is the creation of a new strategic partnership. It also confirms U.S. confidence in India as a global partner and reflects our appreciation for India's excellent nuclear non-proliferation record, its democratic traditions, and its commitment to tolerance and freedom.

India Civil Nuclear Cooperation: Responding to Critics

20

March 8, 2006

Critics: The U.S.-India civil nuclear cooperation deal will accelerate the nuclear arms race in South Asia.

Counterpoint: This is an historic agreement that brings India into the non-proliferation mainstream and addresses its growing energy needs through increased use of nuclear energy in cooperation with the international community. The United States has no intention of aiding India's nuclear weapons program. India's plan to separate its civilian and military nuclear facilities and programs will allow other nations to cooperate with India's civilian facilities to expand energy production. Those facilities will be under International Atomic Energy Agency (IAEA) safeguards to prevent diversion of technology and materials to India's military program. Greater use of nuclear reactors to produce energy for the Indian people will not undermine regional security or stability.

Critics: Doesn't this initiative effectively recognize India as a nuclear weapons state?

Counterpoint: No, the United States has not recognized India as a nuclear weapons state. The 1968 Nuclear Non-Proliferation Treaty (NPT) defines a nuclear weapons state as "one which has manufactured and exploded a nuclear weapon or other nuclear explosive device prior to January 1, 1967." (The United States, UK, France, Russia, and China exploded nuclear devices prior to that date.) India does not meet this definition, and we do not seek to amend the Treaty.

Critics: Only 14 of India's 22 nuclear power reactors will be safeguarded under its separation plan, and India's two developmental fast breeder reactors will remain unsafeguarded.

With these facilities, India can produce enough nuclear weapons to significantly expand its current arsenal.

Counterpoint: The understanding we have reached with India will significantly increase the number of Indian nuclear reactors under IAEA safeguards, as well as bring associated facilities under safeguards. At present, only four of India's nuclear power reactors are under safeguards. Under its civil-military separation plan, India has agreed to place the majority of its existing nuclear power reactors and those under construction under safeguards and to place the other associated upstream and downstream facilities that support those reactors under safeguards. Furthermore, India has committed to place all future civilian power and fast breeder reactors under safeguards.

This agreement is good for American security because it will bring India's civilian nuclear program into the international non-proliferation mainstream. The agreement also is good for the American economy because it will help meet India's surging energy needs—and that will lessen India's growing demand for other energy supplies and help restrain energy prices for American consumers.

Critics: Doesn't this initiative create a double standard and won't it encourage rogue nations like North Korea and Iran to continue to pursue nuclear weapons programs?

Counterpoint: It is not credible to compare the rogue regimes of North Korea and Iran to India. Unlike Iran or North Korea, India has been a peaceful and vibrant democracy with a strong nuclear non-proliferation record.

Under this initiative, India—which has never been a party to the NPT—has agreed to take a series of steps that will bring it into the international non-proliferation mainstream.

Iran and North Korea are very different cases. They signed and ratified the NPT and gave lip service to adhering to their international obligations. Through their covert actions, however, they broke the very non-proliferation commitments they claimed to follow. Additionally, both regimes have isolated themselves from the international community and are state sponsors of terrorism.

India, on the other hand, has agreed to take steps that will bring it into the non-proliferation mainstream, including:

- Placing its civilian nuclear facilities under IAEA safeguards and monitoring;
- Signing and implementing the Additional Protocol, which allows more extensive inspections by the IAEA;
- Ensuring that its nuclear materials and technologies are secured and prevented from diversion, including its recent passage of a law to create a robust national export control system;
- Refraining from transfers of enrichment and reprocessing technologies to states that do not already possess them and supporting efforts to limit their spread;
- Working to conclude a Fissile Material Cut-off Treaty;
- Continuing its moratorium on nuclear testing; and
- Adhering to the Missile Technology Control Regime (MTCR) and the Nuclear Suppliers Group (NSG) guidelines.

Critics: This initiative will weaken or unravel the global non-proliferation regime. Creating an exception for India will lead Pakistan and Israel, who are also outside the NPT regime, to insist on a similar deal or cause other nations to withdraw from the Treaty.

Counterpoint: India has stood outside the global non-proliferation regime for the last 30 years. Through this initiative, India will enter the international non-proliferation mainstream, thereby strengthening the regime that continues to play a vital role in enhancing international security and stability.

All nations that are party to the NPT are permitted full access to nuclear technology for peaceful purposes but are prohibited from pursuing or possessing nuclear weapons (except for the five recognized nuclear weapons states). We do not expect nations to withdraw from the NPT. Any move to withdraw from the NPT would clearly signal a nation's intent to pursue nuclear weapons and would result in the loss of access to nuclear technology for peaceful purposes.

Pakistan and India are different countries with different needs and different histories. Our relationship with Pakistan, which has Major Non-NATO Ally status, follows a separate path that reflects our countries' strong commitment to maintaining close ties and cooperation, including in the War on Terror. However, Pakistan does not have the same non-proliferation record as India, nor the same energy needs. We do not intend to pursue a similar civil nuclear cooperation initiative with Pakistan.

The status of Israel is not comparable to that of India. Israel has not declared itself to be a nuclear power, nor articulated such extraordinary energy needs. As for other Middle Eastern countries, we expect all NPT parties to live up to their Treaty obligations.

21

Suo-Moto Statement by Prime Minister Dr. Manmohan Singh on Discussions on Civil Nuclear Energy Cooperation with the U.S.: Implementation of India's Separation Plan

March 7, 2006

In my Statement on February 27, 2006, I had provided an assurance that this august House will be informed of developments in our discussions with the United States on separation of our civilian and military nuclear facilities. I now inform this august House of developments since my suo motu statement of 27 February.

The President of the United States, His Excellency Mr. George W. Bush visited India between March 1-3, 2006. His visit provided our two countries an opportunity to review progress made in deepening our strategic partnership since the Joint Statement issued during my visit to Washington last July. Our discussions covered the expansion of our ties in the fields of agriculture, economic and trade cooperation, energy security and clean environment, strengthening innovation and the knowledge economy, issues relating to global safety and security and on deepening democracy. Expanded cooperation in each of these areas will have a significant impact on India's social and economic development. The full text of the Joint Statement issued during President Bush's visit is placed on the Table of the House.

I have pleasure in informing the House that during President Bush's visit, as part of the process of promoting cooperation in civilian nuclear energy, agreement was reached between India and the United States on a separation plan. Accordingly, India will identify and separate its civilian and military nuclear facilities and place its civilian nuclear facilities under IAEA safeguards. Sir, I place on the Table of the House the separation plan that has been drawn up by India and agreed between India and the United States in implementation of the India-United States Joint Statement of July 18, 2005.

I would like to outline some salient elements of the separation plan:

(i) India will identify and offer for IAEA safeguards 14 thermal power reactors between 2006-14. There are 22 thermal power reactors in operation or currently under construction in the country. Fourteen of these will be placed under safeguards by 2014 in a phased manner. This would raise the total installed thermal power capacity in Megawatts under safeguards from 19 per cent at present to 65 per cent by 2014. I wish to emphasize that the choice of specific nuclear reactors and the phases in which they would be placed under safeguards is an Indian decision. We are preparing a list of 14 reactors that would be offered for safeguards between 2006-14.

(ii) We have conveyed that India will not accept safeguards on the Prototype Fast Breeder Reactor (PFBR) and the Fast Breeder Test Reactor (FBTR), both located at Kalpakkam. The Fast Breeder Program is at the R&D stage. This technology will take time to mature and reach an advanced stage of development. We do not wish to place any encumbrances on our Fast Breeder program, and this has been fully ensured in the separation plan.

(iii) India has decided to place under safeguards all future civilian thermal power reactors and civilian breeder reactors, and the Government of India retains the sole right to determine such reactors as civilian. This means that India will not be constrained in any way in building future nuclear facilities, whether civilian or military, as per our national requirements.

(iv) India has decided to permanently shut down the CIRUS reactor, in 2010. The fuel core of the Apsara reactor was purchased from France, and we are prepared to shift it from its present location and make it available for placing under safeguards in 2010. Both CIRUS and Apsara are located at the Bhabha Atomic Research Centre. We have decided to take these steps rather than allow intrusive inspections in a nuclear facility of high national security importance. We are determined that such steps will not hinder ongoing Research and Development.

(v) Reprocessing and enrichment capabilities and other facilities associated with the fuel cycle for our strategic programme have been kept out of the separation plan.

(vi) One of the major points addressed in the separation plan was the need to ensure reliability of fuel supplies, given our unfortunate past experience with regard to interruption in supply of fuel for Tarapur. We have received commitments from the United States for the reliable supply of fuel to India for reactors that will be offered for safeguards. The United States has also reaffirmed its assurance to create the necessary conditions for India to have assured and full access to fuel for such reactors. Under the July 18 Joint Statement, the United States is committed to seeking agreement from its Congress to amend domestic laws and to work with friends and allies to adjust the practices of the Nuclear Suppliers Group to create the necessary conditions for India to obtain full access to the international market for nuclear fuel, including reliable, uninterrupted and continual access to fuel supplies from firms in several nations. This has been reflected in the formal understandings reached during the visit and included in the separation plan.

(vii) To further guard against any disruption of fuel supplies for India, the United States is prepared to take other additional steps, such as:

(a) Incorporating assurances regarding fuel supply in a bilateral U.S.-India agreement on peaceful uses of nuclear energy which would be negotiated;

(b) The United States will join India in seeking to negotiate with the IAEA an India-specific fuel supply agreement;

(c) The United States will support an Indian effort to develop a strategic reserve of nuclear fuel to guard against any disruption of supply over the lifetime of India's reactors;

(d) If despite these arrangements, a disruption of fuel supplies to India occurs, the United States and India would jointly convene a group of friendly supplier countries to include countries such as Russia, France and the United Kingdom to pursue such measures as would restore fuel supply to India.

In light of the above understandings with the United States, an India-specific safeguards agreement will be negotiated between India and the IAEA. In essence, an India-specific safeguards agreement would provide: on the one hand safeguards against withdrawal of safeguarded nuclear material from civilian use at any time, and on the other permit India to take corrective measures to ensure uninterrupted operation of its civilian nuclear reactors in the event of disruption of foreign fuel supplies. Taking this into account, India will place its civilian nuclear facilities under India-specific safeguards in perpetuity and negotiate an appropriate safeguards agreement to this end with the IAEA. In the terms of the separation plan, there is hence assurance of uninterrupted supply of fuel to reactors that would be placed under safeguards together with India's right to take corrective measures in the event fuel supplies are interrupted. The House can rest assured that India retains its sovereign right to take all appropriate measures to fully safeguard its interests.

During my suo moto statements on this subject made on July 29, 2005 and on February 27, 2006, I had given a solemn assurance to this august House and through the honorable members to the country, that the separation plan will not adversely affect our country's national security. I am in a position to assure the Members that that this is indeed the case. I might mention:

(i) that the separation plan will not adversely affect our strategic program. There will be no capping of our strategic program, and the separation plan ensures adequacy of fissile material and other inputs to meet the current and future requirements of our strategic program, based on our assessment of the threat scenarios. No constraint has been placed on our right to construct new facilities for strategic purposes. The integrity of our Nuclear Doctrine and our ability to sustain a minimum credible nuclear deterrent is adequately protected. Our nuclear policy will continue to be guided by the principles of restraint and responsibility.

ii) The separation plan does not come in the way of the integrity of our three stage nuclear program, including the future use of our thorium reserves. The autonomy of our Research and Development activities in the nuclear field will remain unaffected. The Fast Breeder Test Reactor and the Prototype Fast Breeder Reactor remain outside safeguards. We have agreed, however, that future civilian Thermal power reactors and civilian Fast Breeder Reactors would be placed under safeguards, but the determination of what is civilian is solely an Indian decision.

As I mentioned in my Statement on February 27, the separation plan has been very carefully drawn up after an intensive internal consultation process overseen by my office. The Department of Atomic Energy and our nuclear scientific community have been associated with the preparation of the separation plan. The Chairman of the Atomic Energy Commission and the Principal Scientific Adviser to the Government of India were actively involved closely at every stage. I am in a position to assure the hon'ble members that we have not permitted information of national security significance to be compromised in any way during the negotiations.

I believe that the significance of the July 18, 2005 Statement is the prospect it offers for ending India's nuclear isolation. It will open up prospects for cooperation not only with the U.S. but with countries like Russia, France and other countries with advanced nuclear capabilities, including those from the NSG. The scope for cooperation in the energy related research will vastly expand, so will cooperation in nuclear research activities. India will be able to join the international mainstream and occupy its rightful place among the top countries of the nuclear community. There would be a quantum jump in our energy generating capacity with a consequential impact on our GDP growth. It also ensures India's participation as a full partner in cutting edge multilateral scientific effort in the nuclear field such as ITER and Generation IV Initiative.

Sir, successful implementation of the July 18 Joint Statement requires reciprocal actions by the United States as well as India. Steps to be taken by India will be contingent upon actions taken by the U.S. For our part, we have prepared a separation plan that identifies those civilian facilities that we are willing to offer for safeguards. The United States Government has accepted this separation plan. It now intends to approach the U.S. Congress for amending its laws and the Nuclear Suppliers Group for adapting its guidelines to enable full civilian cooperation between India and the international community. At the appropriate stage, India will approach the IAEA to discuss and fashion an India-specific safeguards agreement, which will reflect the unique character of this arrangement. Since such a safeguards agreement is yet to be negotiated it will be difficult to predict its content, but I can assure the House that we will not accept any provisions that go beyond the parameters of the July 18, 2005 Statement and the separation plan agreed between India and the United States, on March 2, 2006.We are hopeful that this process will move forward in the coming weeks and months.

I would request hon'ble members to look at this matter through the larger perspective of energy security. Currently, nuclear energy provides only three per cent of our total energy mix. Rising costs and reliability of imported hydrocarbon supplies constitute a major uncertainty at a time when we are accelerating our growth rate. We must endeavor to expand our capabilities across the entire energy spectrum from clean coal and coal-bed methane, to gas hydrates and wind and solar power. We are actively seeking international partnerships across the board and are members of many international initiatives dedicated to energy. Indeed, at the end of my talks with President Bush, we announced Indian participation in two more programs: the FutureGen program for zero emission thermal power plants and the Integrated Ocean Drilling Programme for gas hydrates.

The House will appreciate that the search for an integrated policy with an appropriate mix of energy supplies is central to the achievement of our broader economic or social objectives. Energy is the lifeblood of our economy. Without sufficient and predictable access, our aspirations in the social sector cannot be realized. Inadequate power has a deleterious effect in building a modern infrastructure. It has a direct impact on the optimal usage of increasingly scarce water resources. Power shortage is thus not just a handicap in one sector but a drag on the entire economy.

I believe that the needs of the people of India must become the central agenda for our international cooperation. It is precisely this approach that has guided our growing partnership with the United States. I would, in particular, draw attention to the launching of the Knowledge Initiative in Agriculture with a three year financial commitment to link our universities and technical institutions and businesses to support agricultural education, research, capacity-building, including in the area of bio-technology. Our first Green Revolution benefited in substantial measure from assistance provided by the US. We are hopeful that the Knowledge Initiative on Agriculture will become the harbinger of a second Green Revolution in our country.

Sir, India and the United States have much to gain from this new partnership. This was the main underlying theme of our discussions during the visit of President Bush. The resumption of civilian nuclear energy cooperation would demonstrate that we have entered a new and more positive phase of our ties, so that we can finally put behind us years of troubled relations in the nuclear field. I am confident that this is a worthy objective that will receive the full support of this House.

India and Pakistan: On the Heels of President Bush's Visit

22

R. Nicholas Burns, Under Secretary for Political Affairs

March 6, 2006

U.S.–India Civil Nuclear Agreement

Of course, most of the attention on this trip went to the new civil nuclear agreement. We're very proud of this agreement. We believe it's good for the United States, and we're certain that it's good for India. Essentially, we are looking to bring India into the non-proliferation mainstream, and we're looking to increase the international inspection of India's nuclear facilities and the safeguards that would be applied by the International Atomic Energy Agency to India's civil nuclear power industry.

India has made a number of commitments to us in the agreement we reached on Thursday morning. India has agreed to place 14 of its 22 power reactors under international safeguards. That represents roughly 66 per cent of its current capacity. India has also agreed that all of its future civil thermal and civil breeder reactors—all of them—will be put under safeguards as they are constructed.

India agreed as well that the safeguards to be put in place will be done in perpetuity, meaning these will be permanent safeguards. They are not safeguards that will be in place for a number of years and taken off at the convenience of the Indian Government. They'll be permanently in place. India has agreed to extend its moratorium on nuclear testing. India has, of course, passed last June landmark export control legislation on weapons of mass destruction.

So in all these areas, we think that India has made commitments, not only to the United States in this plan it is putting forward today, but to the international community, which allow India for the very first time in the life of its nuclear program (over 30 years) to be able to submit itself in a transparent way for international inspection.

We think that's a major, major gain for the non-proliferation community. In return, what we in the United States—and what our friends and allies around the world—will do is to try to seek change through law, and we will ask the Congress to consider that. This will be up to the Congress. And we will ask the Nuclear Suppliers Group to adjust its practices so that civil trade on the part of all of our countries and our companies with India will in the future be possible—meaning investment in the nuclear power industry in India and the transfer of technology, which India has been lacking for the 30 years of its nuclear program.

We believe that in the future, India is going to face enormous energy needs. It's a country, as all of you know, of just over a billion people. It will soon be the most populous nation on earth. Its economy has been growing at a rate of 8 per cent to 9 per cent per year, and the forecasts are that it will continue or even increase in the years ahead. India, like China, has enormous civil, peaceful power needs. One of the ways that India hopes to address that need is to increase its civil nuclear power production. We understand that the vast growth in the future of the nuclear industry in India is going to be in civil nuclear power, with the construction of 1,000-megawatt power plants to help provide electricity to Indians in the cities and in the rural parts of the country.

So if you look at the agreement that we made with the Indian Government, it's very likely that the great majority of the future growth will be on the civilian side. India has pledged that all of the thermal and breeder reactors that are civilian will come under safeguards, and we expect that the percentage of India's nuclear power industry that will eventually come under international safeguards is going to increase from that 66 per cent figure to a figure much broader than that by the year 2020.

It's not up to me to announce India's intentions in this regard in terms of how many power plants will come on line.

That's a function, a responsibility of the Indian Government. But we're convinced that one of the most important aspects of this deal is not just how much India is offering to do today, but if you look at the future growth on the civilian side, an ever-increasing percentage of its nuclear industry will come under safeguards because the great majority of new construction will be and has to be, given the energy needs of the country in the civil nuclear field.

Obviously, this was an important part of what the President set out to do. The negotiations that we have with the Indian government extended from roughly last April, April 2005, until last Thursday. They were difficult negotiations, and as President Bush said in his press conference in Delhi on Thursday, we understand how difficult it was for the Indian Government to come to this agreement. It was also difficult for us. After all, the United States very firmly believes in the Non-Proliferation Treaty. We will not recognize, as part of this deal, India as a nuclear weapons power. We are simply trying to make space for India in the international non-proliferation realm to bring them into the system so that they could, after 30 years of isolation, participate, gain the advantages of that system, but also submit themselves in a responsible way to oversight and to inspections and to transparency that the IAEA is going to demand. We think, on balance, that is a powerful move forward for India, for the United States, and for the world, and we're convinced that it's the right step forward.

What the President and Secretary Rice will be doing over the next week or two is to talk to Members of Congress, in the House and the Senate, to describe in some detail the arrangement that was negotiated just last week, and we will now respectfully submit a request to Congress that U.S. law might be changed so that American companies will be able to participate in the expansion of India's civil nuclear power facility.

The executive branch, in essence, has done the job we set out to do in negotiating and agreeing to this initiative. But in our system of government—and I think this is very well understood by the Indian public and by the Indian press—in our system of government, only Congress can change U.S. law. And so we hope very much to receive the support of the Congress. I wouldn't want to anticipate what the Congress will do. I think there's a respect for the separation of powers here, and we very much respect the role of Congress. We'll be trying to do the best job we can in convincing Congress this is a good deal for American interests....

23

President Discusses Strong U.S.-India Partnership in New Delhi, India

President George W. Bush
March 3, 2006

....By leading together, America and India can meet other global challenges, and one of the biggest is energy. Like America, India's growing economy requires growing amounts of electricity. And the cleanest and most reliable way to meet that need is through civilian nuclear power. Last summer in Washington, America and India reached an agreement to share civilian nuclear technology and to bring India's civilian nuclear programs under the safeguards of the International Atomic Agency. In our meetings this week, Palestinian representative, Singh and I agreed on a plan to implement this historic initiative. Our agreement will strengthen the security and the economy of both our nations. (Applause.)

By applying the most advanced technology and international standards to India's civilian nuclear program, we will increase safety and reduce the risk of proliferation. And by helping India meet its energy needs, we will take the pressure off the price of fossil fuels for consumers in India and America and around the world. We'll help India be good stewards of our environment, and we will strengthen the bonds of trust between our two great nations. (Applause.)...

24 Under Secretary Burns: Press Briefing in India

R. Nicholas Burns, Under Secretary of State for Political Affairs

March 2, 2006

Under Secretary Burns: Good afternoon. I'll be happy to say a few words about the civil nuclear agreement that was agreed to today by President Bush and Prime Minister Singh. Let me just take you through that agreement, what it says, why we decided to initiate it, and then I'll be happy to answer your questions.

We believe that this agreement represents a historic step forward for both India and the United States. In its largest sense, in the geopolitical sense, the agreement today removes a basic irritant in the relations between India and the United States over the last 30 years and allows both of our countries now to engage in a high degree of civil nuclear energy cooperation for the future.

I think there are two main benefits of the agreement—the first concerns non-proliferation. For 30 years India has been outside the international non-proliferation system. It's been under sanction; it's not been allowed to trade in civil nuclear energy technology for its nuclear power structure—its civil nuclear power structure—with any other country. And India has agreed in this initiative that it will open up its system to international inspection. And we have agreed that Western—American firms and other firms will be able to invest in India's nuclear technology.

The gain for non-proliferation is that we have never had a way to have an impact, even insight, a transparent insight into India's nuclear program; now we will have that. There's a second—and a secondary gain, and that is that full civil nuclear trade will ensue. And that means that there will be opportunities for American firms, as well as other firms, to bring the latest in technology in the nuclear power industry to the nuclear establishment here in India.

As you know, as the Prime Minister talked about this morning, the President did, as well, energy is one of the major issues here affecting India's future growth. It's a country of a billion people; it has enormous energy requirements. Nuclear power, civil nuclear power is not going to be the panacea to address that problem, but it's a major part of it.

The understanding that we reached today with the Indians was reached after eight months of negotiation. You'll remember that President Bush and Secretary Rice set out the vision in the spring of 2005 that we ought to find a way forward to begin, after 30 years, a new relationship in civil nuclear energy. When the Prime Minister visited the White House on July 18, 2005, there was a basic agreement that we would head in this direction, but that agreement had to be filled out, it had to be written down, and it, effectively, had to be implemented, and so we had eight months of negotiations, very intensive negotiations, both here in India, in the United States, in countries in between, and those negotiations finished this morning, which allowed the President and Prime Minister to make their announcement.

The practical aspect is this: India has agreed as of this—because of this agreement to open up a majority of its nuclear power reactors and its associated nuclear facilities to permanent IAEA—International Atomic Energy Agency—safeguards. Since the establishment of the Indian nuclear program in 1974, there has been no international oversight, and now the majority of India's program will be under supervision of the International Agency.

Second, India, for the very first time in 30 years, has accepted new non-proliferation obligations. It has now passed a national export control law, which will bring its legal requirements into international conformance. It has committed to refrain from transferring any of its nuclear technologies. It has reasserted its commitment to maintain a unilateral moratorium of nuclear testing, and it has agreed to work with the United States towards a fissile material cut-off treaty. These are gains that were not possible during any time over the last 30 years; they are made possible by this agreement today.

The practical vehicle for this initiative was for India to have developed over the last eight months a plan to separate its military facilities in the nuclear field and its civil facilities. And that plan was accepted by the United States this morning. We now believe that there will be two initiatives that we have to undertake to regularize this agreement. Firstly, the President will have to approach the Congress to ask for a change in U.S. law, specifically, modifications to the Atomic Energy Act of 1954, and the way in which it was modified in 1978. And we hope very much, in working with Congress, that we'll be able to convince the Congress to move forward and change American law.

Secondly, India will approach the IAEA and the Nuclear Suppliers Group, along with the United States, to see a change in international practice. And that will allow other countries around the world to do what the United States has done, and that is to initiate trade in civil nuclear energy. I expect both of those initiatives, our legislation in the United States and the international practice in the NSG to be initiated fairly soon.

I would also say that this initiative we expect will have strong support from the international community. A number of countries have already spoken out in favor of this initiative. Dr. ElBaradei, the Chairman and the Nobel laureate of the IAEA, has indicated that he is in support of this deal. He has said that to us in meetings over the last few months. And a number of our allies in Europe, the Russian government, have all said that they would favor this initiative. So we do expect broad-scale international support.

This represents the culmination of a year of American diplomacy, and this deal very much symbolizes the larger meaning of the President's visit, which is, as he said in his press conference today, the creation of a new strategic relationship between India and the United States. This is not the only part of that, it's a highly symbolic part of it, but it coincides with the initiatives we've made today in agriculture, and science and technology, in the defense field, in space cooperation. That, for the first time since 1947, mean that India and the United States will have a fully diverse and very broad economic, technological and scientific cooperation.

I know that some of you were interested in some of the questions that were asked about how does this deal intersect with the larger non-proliferation concerns that we have globally. What distinguishes India is that India has protected its nuclear technology over the 30 years of the India nuclear program. India has not proliferated, unlike North Korea, which has been a major proliferator. India has brought itself into conformance with all the international guidelines pertaining to nuclear technology, unlike Iran, for instance, which has been a great violator of those international programs. So we could not have made this deal with any country that had proliferated, that had been acting contrary to the international proliferation system. We can make it with India because India has been a good steward of its own nuclear materials.

So with that, I'll be happy to take any questions. Terry.

Question: Nick, how many civilian and nuclear reactors, how did they divide that up? How many did they decide to put in each classification? And did they accept the thing that Secretary Rice was talking about yesterday—about the classification would have to be forever, that they couldn't move from one to the other?

Under Secretary Burns: I think I'll leave it to the Indian government to announce exactly how many of its nuclear power plants are being put under supervision. I think it's only right that I do that. But I can tell you....

Question: Well, you're part of the agreement.

Under Secretary Burns: I can tell you that a majority of India's nuclear power plants will be put under international safeguards, and that they will be permanent safeguards—what we call safeguards in perpetuity. That's very important. That is a signal both to the United States and to the rest of the international community that this move by the Indian Government is permanent. It's going to be sustainable and it's not going to be taken back. And I think Secretary Rice said the other day on Air Force One that she felt it was very important that these be permanent—and they are.

I should also tell you that India has agreed that in the future all of its future civilian power reactors, thermal reactors and breeder reactors, will be placed under international safeguards. I think when we started out in this agreement nearly a year ago, there was some doubt that we'd be able to achieve a comprehensive agreement that would place the breeder reactors in the future—future civilian breeder reactors under safeguards. But that is the commitment that the India government made to us today.

So let's just recap what happened, what the Indian government did. They said they'll put a majority of their civil nuclear power reactors under safeguards, and that will be phased in between 2006 and 2014. Secondly, they said that in the future, as they construct nuclear power plants, all the civil thermal and breeder reactors will be put under safeguards.

Thirdly, they said that they would enter into permanent safeguard arrangements with the International Atomic Energy Agency. We have now achieved a degree of transparency and oversight and impact on the Indian nuclear program that was not possible for three decades. So, from a non-proliferation standpoint, this is a major win for the United States, as well as for India. And from an economic standpoint, it's going to open up a major expansion of American civil trade on the part of our companies with the Indian nuclear establishment.

Question: Does this restrict in any way India's production of fissile material or the number of weapons that it can produce?

Under Secretary Burns: The one thing we have not done in agreeing to this initiative today is to formally recognize India as a nuclear weapon state. The United States does not do that, as you know. But the agreement will cover the majority of Indian civil nuclear industry, but India will continue, obviously, with its strategic program. And the agreement doesn't—will not have an impact on that strategic program, as you described it.

Question: Will future reactors, those fast breeder reactors, will they be permanently placed under safeguards? Is that permanent, forever?

Under Secretary Burns: Yes. One of the Indian commitments is that those future thermal power reactors, as well as breeder reactors that are classified as civilian will be put under permanent IAEA safeguards. I think it's fair to say that anyone looking at the Indian nuclear program since 1974, when it was initiated, would have been—would not have predicted that India would open itself up to such a large degree. Now, India has done so because it wants to emerge from the isolation of the last three decades, it wants to re-enter the international non-proliferation mainstream—and that's what this agreement allows it to do. It allows all of us that are partners of India now to have an oversight of that system that will help stem the proliferation of nuclear materials. So we're very pleased about it from that perspective.

Question: How late were you negotiating this morning?

Under Secretary Burns: Pardon?

Question: How late did you negotiate?

Under Secretary Burns: The negotiations lasted from last July until about 10:30 a.m. this morning. Now, you can imagine how complex this was. What the Indians did after Prime Minister Singh's visit to the White House in July was to develop a plan, a very complex plan that would, in effect, separate its military nuclear facilities and its civilian nuclear facilities. And we helped the Indians to try to think through the separation of that plan, because it has to be presented to the United States Congress and then it will have to be presented to the Nuclear Suppliers Group.

And the President, of course, had the vision that we would achieve this agreement. Secretary Rice was engaged in negotiations over the last eight months. A number of us were engaged in—I think we made five trips here, and last evening, Steve Hadley and I and others met with the Indians until around midnight. We met again this morning. And the Prime Minister and the President, of course, made the final agreement on behalf of both countries.

Question: The United States had been maintaining very strongly that the breeder programs be also included. So the fact that now the breeder programs are not being included immediately, what are the chances that cooperation may not occur?

Under Secretary Burns: Well, India has never been a proliferator of its nuclear technology. We would not have made this agreement had India been a different kind of country, firstly. Secondly, India has a very limited capacity now—one prototype breeder reactor and one test reactor. It seeks to build a much larger capacity and it's made a commitment that its future civilian breeder reactors will all come under safeguards.

As we talked to our friends around the world, in Europe and in Asia, about this agreement, this was an abiding concern that any final agreement include breeder reactors, and this agreement does include breeder reactors.

Question: Not immediately, right?

Under Secretary Burns: Well, as those reactors are built and they're classified to be civilian, they'll come under safeguards. India right now derives a very small percentage of its total energy requirements from nuclear energy. What it wants to do, like many other countries, is to build up substantially its nuclear—its peaceful nuclear energy program. And the commitment today is that as that sector is built up, the large percentage of it is going to come under safeguards.

Question: You're using the word "majority." Did India actually agree to specific numbers and specific locations?

Under Secretary Burns: It did. I think I'm just constrained by the rules of diplomatic nicety not to make an announcement on behalf of the Indian Government. So you'll ask them. And I think they have to report to their parliament. But I can tell you that a substantial majority of India's nuclear facilities will come under safeguards, both by numbers of reactors and by percentage of total mega-wattage power. Those are the two metrics that one uses to judge this agreement.

Question: But were there items that you actually just agreed to put off because you wanted for them to be able to announce an agreement today?

Under Secretary Burns: Well, I think it's—the plan that was under discussion is an Indian Government plan to separate its civil and military nuclear facilities. It's not a U.S. Government plan. But as we are a partner of India in trying to both change American law to permit this kind of cooperation, and also international practice, we had a lot to do with the negotiations. And I just don't think it would be right for me to announce a specific number when that's the Government of India's responsibility and business. But I can describe the agreement to you in general, and we think it's a substantial one.

Question:—India never start taking this agreement—China and Pakistan, because recently General Musharraf also said that if India is getting this from the U.S., why not Pakistan.

Under Secretary Burns: We have always seen this deal to be a unique deal for India alone. We do not believe this deal should be or will be replicated by the United States for other countries that are outside the non-proliferation mainstream. We certainly would never consider entertaining this with a country that proliferated—for instance, North Korea; or a country that had lied to the IAEA—Iran. And of course, despite our friendship for Pakistan, there have been proliferation problems of a quite serious nature over the last several years that would make this kind of deal impossible, and we've been very upfront and direct with the Pakistanis in saying that.

India is unique. It is soon to be the largest country in the world by population. It is a country now where the United States is the largest investor and the largest trade partner. It has a growing need for energy. It has a growing interest in developing peaceful nuclear energy. It had developed its entire nuclear program over 30 years alone because it had been isolated. So the question that we faced was the following: Is it better to maintain India in isolation, or is it better to try to bring it into the international mainstream? And President Bush felt the latter, that we ought to try to bring India into compliance actively, with the major international agreements that govern the disposition of nuclear materials, for instance, and nuclear energy.

It's not a perfect deal in the sense that we haven't captured 100 per cent of India's nuclear program. That's because India is a nuclear weapons power, and India will preserve part of its nuclear industry to service its nuclear weapons program. But the majority of the program will now come under international inspection. And we think that is a tremendous and positive gain for us.

Question: The President said earlier today that it was a new way of thinking, a new way of doing business. So you're saying that this is very much India-specific, this is not to be considered a model for perhaps other countries who would like to arrange a similar deal?

Under Secretary Burns: The President—what the President has said was a new way of doing business certainly with India—and it is. Because the conventional wisdom on India for three decades had been because India's nuclear program grew outside the purview of the Non-Proliferation Treaty, India should be isolated. And we felt that since India had been so uniquely responsible in not proliferating, and that while it was not officially part of these international regimes, it was in compliance with most of the norms of the regimes, we felt it made a lot of sense to try to regularize this process and bring them into the system.

And so that was the vision that we had a year ago. The challenge was in translating it into a specific agreement, and that's what we've worked on for the better part of the last year. So, in essence, what this deal has always been about is that in return for international inspection of its civil nuclear energy facilities, we—the United States and other countries —will agree for the first time to engage in trade and investment into that nuclear power system. And we think that's a good deal for both sides.

Question: What's going to be the congressional landscape towards this, the way you see the pockets of resistance? And also, the President this morning talked about a good-faith gesture by the Indians—what was he referring to?

Under Secretary Burns: I think in terms of Congress, obviously, Congress will now play the key role. The executive branch, of course, has had the initiative to make the deal, but this deal requires a change in United States law, and Congress obviously will have to do that.

We have kept members of Congress well-informed throughout the last eight months. There have been a number of formal hearings in the House and the Senate. There have been lots of private briefings, including many last week, and we hope very much that Congress, both in the House and Senate, will now see that this deal is a gain for the U.S. and a gain for non-proliferation, and that U.S. law might be changed.

I know that there are some detractors on Capitol Hill who have said that they will oppose this legislation. There are many members of the House and Senate who say they will support it. And there are other members who have been waiting to see the specifics of the separation plan and of the agreement we reached today, and we'll begin briefing Congress later on this afternoon. I know Secretary Rice will be making phone calls. She hopes to call Senator Lugar and Chairman Hyde, the relevant committee chairs, and we'll call all the other members of Congress—and there are a lot of them who are interested in this agreement.

Question: Nick, you said the majority, and you said you can't tell exactly how many. Can you tell us what percentage?

Under Secretary Burns: Well, I can tell you that the Prime Minister spoke to parliament on Monday evening, and he announced that 60—I believe 65 of India's overall power sector would come under civilian safeguards.

Question: Would that be—

Under Secretary Burns: Well, that's the figure he announced.

Question: What percentage of that is—

Under Secretary Burns: Of total mega-wattage.

Question: Well, what is the percentage of—if 100 per cent is everything, what does 65 represent? What per cent of India's—

Under Secretary Burns: Of its total power production. Yes.

Question: Sixty-five per cent?

Under Secretary Burns: Sixty-five per cent will come under safeguards, of its nuclear power production. Now, you might also be asking, how many reactors will come under safeguards, and that really is for the Indian Government to announce. I think they will shortly.

Question: Secretary Burns, there was a report just now on CNN that 14 nuclear reactors will come under scrutiny. Is that correct?

Under Secretary Burns: Well, I wouldn't argue. I can't—I wouldn't argue against that figure, but it's not for me to announce it.

Question: Can I ask two questions that I think maybe are related? One is, are there business opportunities for the U.S. outside strictly the nuclear production, nuclear power area embraced in the agreement that you reached today? The other question is, are there—is it possible for there to be non-civilian breeder reactors that they would build in the future?

Under Secretary Burns: The answer to the second question is yes, India could build reactors that would service their nuclear weapons industry. It is much more likely, however, that the great percentage of the growth in the nuclear industry is going to be civilian, because the major strategic desire of the government is to increase power output, electricity generation for this enormous country. And so the answer is, yes, they could build facilities to service the nuclear weapons program, but the great majority of the growth we think will come on the civilian side.

Question: Are there business opportunities outside the nuclear power production area for the United States?

Under Secretary Burns: In the nuclear field or in general?

Question: In this sort of—the gamut of agreements that you've reached here today.

Under Secretary Burns: Yes, and I think Steve Hadley is coming to brief on the rest of the initiatives. But, in short, if you look at—have seen the joint statement that's going to be issued, there are major initiatives in agriculture, in science and technology, in energy, in education, in space cooperation—substantial agreements. And if you will, as in July, what we are announcing today is a major expansion in 16 or 17 different areas of U.S.-Indian cooperation across the board. I think everybody agrees, everybody on both sides of this relationship, that we've never had as good a relationship between our countries at any time since 1947, since India's independence, and that we've never had as broad an engagement in terms of our economic trade and investment, and our foreign policy cooperation, as we have now. So I think most of us feel, in the American and Indian governments, this is now the high water mark of U.S.-India relations over the last 60 years.

Question: Did the two leaders play any direct role in resolving unresolved issues that were still hanging out there, or was it basically they just signed off on what you all did?

Under Secretary Burns: They did. They had a discussion in the Oval Office on July 18th of 2005 which was the key discussion in agreeing to head in this direction. And again this morning, before the agreement was made, the President and Prime Minister had a thorough discussion of the issue. They weren't negotiating the text—that was left to others, of course—but they are the strategic architects of this agreement, there's no question about that.

Question: But there wasn't anything that you had to say, all right, we've got to kick it up to these guys to hash out this little detail?

Under Secretary Burns: The final details were made in other negotiations, the final details were resolved. But, obviously, our instructions came from the President.

Question: Can you verify, in saying that they've committed to all future civilian breeder reactors being part of this power program, IAEA program, that that would anticipate the possibility of a future breeder reactor being built for the military?

Under Secretary Burns: Yes, I answered in the affirmative.

Question: And the existing prototype breeder reactor stays in the military program?

Under Secretary Burns: That's up to the Indians to decide. They have a choice of maintaining that in the miliary sphere, or it could transition to the civil sphere.

Here's a prediction. India has had to develop its entire program on its own, for the reasons that, as well, are well-known to everyone. When and if it's now possible for international investment and trade in nuclear materials and nuclear fuel and nuclear power plant technology with India, there's going to be a great incentive on the part of the Indians to have as much in the civil side of their nuclear structure as possible, because it will only be possible for American firms, French firms, Russian firms, to invest in trade with those reactors and facilities that are under safeguards. If they haven't been placed under safeguards, the minority of India's program, then, of course, the isolation will remain in place. So the incentives are to see a large increase, we think, in the civilian side.

Question: And lastly, in as much as any negotiation is a give and take, is there one significant thing that the United States had to concede here to close this?

Under Secretary Burns: I don't really see it that way, and this was a long negotiation—it was eight months—so it's hard to pick out and say it was decisive. I think for us what was most important was that a majority of India's current nuclear facilities would be put under international inspection, international safeguards—the majority—so that this plan that we announce today would be credible, as well as transparent.

And secondly, it was very important for us that as we look towards the future—because there will be a huge expansion now in the number of power plants in this country—that there would be a commitment that the future civilian power reactors and breeder reactors would all—all—be based under safeguards. And that was agreed to yesterday. And so that was a very significant step forward, and it was critical to our agreement to this initiative.

Question: Does the Indian parliament have to approve this deal?

Under Secretary Burns: I don't—I believe the Indian Prime Minister will be reporting to the parliament, but I don't believe there's any—there's no similar process as the one—because what we have to do now is, as I said, there is a U.S. law which prohibits a private American firm from investing in a nuclear power plant in India, or from selling nuclear fuel to India. And so we will respectfully ask the Congress to amend that law and to make an exception for India—not for a group of other countries, but for India, itself. And that's the Atomic Energy Act of 1954. That was amended in 1978 during the Carter administration. And so that—we would ask the Congress to make an exception and to change U.S. law in that respect.

And the other technical aspect of this, Elisabeth, is that we would then—the administration would submit a bilateral civil nuclear cooperation agreement between India and the United States to the Congress. And then, third, we would—the United States has agreed to go to the Nuclear Suppliers Group—that's the group of 45 countries that are the major suppliers of nuclear fuel and technology for power industries—and we would ask that group, which also prohibits business with India, to remove those restrictions so that other countries—France, Russia, Britain, Japan—would be able to undertake the same kind of trade we are.

So it's going to be an elaborate process, and what the President was announcing today was that we've got an agreement with the Indian Government to go forward, but in our case, we need congressional authorization to be able actually to carry this out.

Question: When you said India for the very first time has agreed to put its reactors under international scrutiny, is it for the first time in history, or the first time in three decades?

Under Secretary Burns: Well, it's for the first time in a long, long time, and it's the first time that a substantial number of these reactors would be under safeguards, and that they would sign an agreement for permanent safeguards at the IAEA itself.

Question: This agreement to refrain from transferring technology for their civilian and military program—does that apply only to imported technology, or to overall?

Under Secretary Burns: No, it applies to all technology, whether it's indigenously produced or whether it's imported. That's a very important point—all technology.

So the way to look at this—and I certainly understand this is a complex and esoteric arrangement—is India has a nuclear program; the majority of what India does is produce power through civil nuclear reactors. A minority of what they do is to use nuclear reactors to produce the elements that are necessary for nuclear weaponry. And what we're saying is that India will have international trade and investment into that civil sector, and the entire civil sector will be opened up to international inspection, but the nuclear weapons sector of their program will not be open to trade and investment, nor safeguards. And so that's going to be walled off. And that's important. The United States has not recognized formally India as a nuclear weapons state, and that's important. But we do recognize the need for nuclear power in this country.

I think it was—we were convinced that we had to make this choice, as the President said today, to think in new ways about how to deal with the largest country in the world, a country that is a friend of ours, that's democratic, that has not proliferated. And the choice was, do we go through another 30 years and just completely isolate them, or do we integrate them into the international system. And we think by doing so today, it is a major step forward in the cause of non-proliferation, and it's a very good example for other countries that if you are an effective steward of your nuclear material, there are rewards.

Contrast that with Iran and North Korea. Both acted against the wishes of the international community, Iran having withheld information from the IAEA for 18 years, and North Korea you know about. So I think if you're looking for examples and lessons in how this has an impact on the international community, the impact's going to be positive, because India has effectively played by the rules, in terms of proliferation.

Question: Mr. Under Secretary, China has already responded by saying that it would rather have India sign the Non-Proliferation Treaty. I guess my question is, I'd like your response on that. The other question is, could you give us a sense of what this civil and nuclear trade could be worth annually for the Nuclear Suppliers Group, or for the United States?

Under Secretary Burns: Well, the main motivation here is non-proliferation; a secondary benefit is economic. That economic benefit is going to be in the billions, there's no question about that, because of the huge nature of the Indian economy and the expansion that they are planning in the civil nuclear energy field. And given the state of technological research on nuclear reactors, and given the elementary ingredient of financing, this is an extremely beneficial proposition—the payoff, the economic benefits, in the long-term, will be substantial, certainly in the billions.

Question:—the China question?

Under Secretary Burns: I haven't seen the Chinese comment, so it's never wise to comment on something you really haven't read or haven't seen someone speak. I would just say this: China is a member of the Nuclear Suppliers Group; most of the major countries of the Nuclear Suppliers Group I think will end up supporting this, and we certainly hope China will, as well.

Question: Mr. Burns, has any assurance been given to India on uninterrupted supply of fuel, of nuclear fuel?

Under Secretary Burns: Yes, the United States—what we did today was to commit to the Indians that we would work very hard to help ensure a continuous and reliable supply of nuclear fuel to India itself.

First of all, we have a bilateral agreement now to negotiate, and we will embed in that bilateral agreement assurances that we will seek to help India secure fuel for its nuclear reactors. Secondly, we have agreed that India and the United States will approach the IAEA for a multilateral regime to supply fuel for India. Thirdly, we've agreed to set up a council of advisors—India and the United States and other countries—so that if there is ever a threat of interruption of supply, those countries could meet to figure out how to maintain supply to India.

We think, frankly, the greatest guarantor of supply of nuclear fuel to India will be the world market. Once U.S. laws change and once international practices are changed, there's going to be a competitive world market wanting to sell fuel—nuclear fuel into India. And so we think that will be continuous and very reliable, and we don't think it should cause a concern for the Indian Government.

Thank you very much.

Fact Sheet: United States and India: Strategic Partnership

25

March 2, 2006

> *"We have an ambitious agenda with India. Our agenda is practical. It builds on a relationship that has never been better. India is a global leader, as well as a good friend.... My trip will remind everybody about the strengthening of an important strategic partnership. We'll work together in practical ways to promote a hopeful future for citizens in both our nations."*
>
> President George W. Bush, February 22, 2006

Civil Nuclear Cooperation: The United States and India have reached an historic agreement on civil nuclear cooperation. The agreement addresses India's surging energy needs for its growing economy. This will also ease the burden on other countries as the world's energy needs continue to rise.

- The U.S. and India have agreed to pursue civil nuclear cooperation to allow India to cooperate and trade in this key area.
- India has agreed to take steps that will bring it into the international non-proliferation mainstream, including placing its civilian nuclear facilities and programs under IAEA safeguards and adhering to the guidelines of the Nuclear Suppliers Group and the Missile Technology Control Regime.

The U.S.-India strategic partnership is rooted in shared values and is broad in nature and scope, with our two countries working together on global issues, including expanding economic freedom and democracy; ensuring plentiful sources of clean, safe, and reliable energy; protecting security; supporting innovation and technological advances; and promoting public health.

Economy: The United States and India are expanding cooperation to enhance job creation and economic growth; support economic reform and liberalization; develop a bilateral business climate supportive of trade and investment; and improve market access for goods and services.

- **Trade:** Over the last five years, U.S. exports to India have more than doubled, helping to create better-paying jobs in the United States. The United States and India agree that trade is essential to promoting global economic growth, development, freedom, and prosperity. Both countries are committed to completing the WTO Doha Development Agenda before the end of 2006.
- **Investment:** The United States and India welcomed the report of the U.S.-India CEO Forum and agreed to work on its recommendations through the Economic Dialogue; endorsed the efforts of the U.S.-India Trade Policy Forum to reduce barriers to trade and investment; agreed to hold a high-level public-private investment summit in 2006; and are continuing the dialogue on various issues, including further liberalization of investment restrictions, regulatory transparency, dispute settlement, and reducing tariff and non-tariff barriers to trade.
- **Agriculture:** The United States and India have launched the Knowledge Initiative on Agriculture to link universities, technical institutions, and businesses to support high-priority joint agriculture education, research, and capacity-building projects including biotechnology.

Democracy: Building on their common values and interests, the United States and India affirmed their joint commitment to promote freedom and democracy and assist countries in transition. Effective democracies with governments accountable to the people are the best means of ensuring long-term stability and prosperity.

- The United States and India will work together to support the growth and development of vibrant civil societies, including independent media and non-governmental organizations, in countries that seek such assistance.

Energy and the Environment: The United States and India are working together to help meet India's rising demand for energy by looking at new technologies to produce clean, safe, and reliable energy.

- **FutureGen:** India will join the FutureGen international partnership which will work to create a zero-emissions coal-fired power plant, enabling greater use of coal in an environmentally sustainable way.
- **International Thermonuclear Experimental Reactor (ITER):** India has joined the United States, Russia, the European Union, Japan, the Republic of Korea, and China as an ITER member.
- **Asia-Pacific Partnership on Clean Development and Climate:** The United States and India, together with Australia, China, Japan, and the Republic of Korea, will work on practical ways to improve energy security, improve air quality, and reduce greenhouse gas emissions in ways that foster economic growth.

Security: The United States and India are building the foundation of a durable defense relationship that will continue to support our common strategic and security interests.

- **Maritime Security Cooperation:** The United States and India are committed to a comprehensive cooperative effort to ensure a secure maritime domain.
- **Counterterrorism:** The United States and India are jointly expanding the scope of our counter-terrorism cooperation, including work on bioterrorism and cybersecurity.
- **Military Logistics Support:** The United States and India will soon sign an agreement to facilitate mutual logistic support during combined training, exercises, and disaster relief operations.

- **Defense Trade:** The United States reaffirmed its goal to help meet India's defence needs and to provide the important technologies and capabilities that India seeks.
- **Non-proliferation:** Both countries support efforts to limit the spread of enrichment and reprocessing technologies and also support the conclusion of a Fissile Material Cut-off Treaty.

Innovative and Advanced Technologies: The United States and India are working together to support the creation of innovative, dynamic, knowledge-based economies.

- **Intellectual Property Rights (IPR):** The United States is funding IPR training programs to strengthen enforcement and patent examination, as a vibrant IPR regime is critical to the promotion of a creative, technologically advanced economy.
- **Science:** The United States and India established and co-fund the $30 million Bi-National Science and Technology Commission to generate collaborative partnerships in science and technology.
- **Space:** The United States and India have agreed to continue exploring further cooperation in civil space, including areas such as space exploration, satellite navigation, and earth science. In addition, agreements are being completed that will allow for the launch of U.S. satellites and satellites containing U.S. components by Indian launch vehicles.

Public Health: The United States and India are cooperating to expand efforts to combat and prevent Avian Influenza and HIV/AIDS.

- **Avian Influenza:** The United States and India agreed to expand bilateral efforts on avian influenza by, among other things, reaching out to the private sector, developing regional communications strategies, and planning an in-region containment and response exercise. India will host the International Partnership on Avian and Pandemic Influenza Meeting in 2007.

- **HIV/AIDS:** Last July, President Bush and Prime Minister Singh agreed to further strengthen cooperation on HIV/AIDS by leveraging resources, knowledge, and expertise. Since then:
  - The United States increased funding in FY2006 for HIV/AIDS prevention, care, and treatment programs to $29.3 million.
  - We have established an Indo-U.S. Corporate Sector Fund for HIV/AIDS, which is a partnership among U.S. and Indian businesses to fight AIDS. Six companies have already pledged a total of $1.2 million to the Fund.
  - The U.S. Food and Drug Administration has given approval to 13 generic antiretroviral drugs produced by Indian pharmaceutical companies. These drugs can now be purchased as part of the President's Emergency Plan for HIV/AIDS for use around the world.

26 Remarks by President Bush and Prime Minister Manmohan Singh of India

President **George W. Bush;** Prime Minister **Manmohan Singh**

March 2, 2006

Prime Minister Singh: Shall I start?

President Bush: Please.

Prime Minister Singh: Mr. President, ladies and gentlemen of the press: President Bush and I have completed very cordial and productive discussions this morning. We reviewed the status of our cooperation, including the agenda that was set on July 18, 2005. The joint statement that will be shared with all of you today contains a number of announcements and initiatives that underline the significant progress in our relationship....

I'm particularly pleased that we have reached an understanding on the implementation of our agreement on civil nuclear cooperation of July 18, 2005. I have conveyed to the President that India has finalized the identification of civilian facilities to which we had committed. I was also happy to hear from the President that he now intended to approach the U.S. Congress to amend U.S. laws and the Nuclear Suppliers Group to adjust its guideline. We will discuss with the International Atomic Energy Agency in regard to fashioning an appropriate India-specific safeguards agreement. You will appreciate I cannot say more now, while our parliament is in session.

Before concluding, I would like to express my warm appreciation for the personal interest shown and the leadership role that President Bush has played in the transformation of our ties. I have met the President a number of times, and on each occasion, I have admired his vision, his resolve, and his commitment to strengthening our bilateral relations. Our discussion today make me confident that there are no limits to the Indo-U.S. partnerships.

May I invite you, Mr. President, now to make your remarks....

President Bush: ....As the Prime Minister mentioned, we concluded an historic agreement today on nuclear power. It's not an easy job for the Prime Minister to achieve this agreement, I understand. It's not easy for the American President to achieve this agreement. But it's a necessary agreement. It's one that will help both our peoples.

Again, I applaud you for your courage and your leadership. I'm looking forward to working with our United States Congress to change decades of law that will enable us to move forward in this important initiative.

Also we talked about the advanced energy initiative that I'm proposing in my own country. Listen, the whole purpose of the advanced energy initiative is to end our dependence on oil, and as we develop technologies that will enable us to do so, we look forward to working with India so we can achieve the same objectives. Dependency upon fossil fuels, particularly during times of shortage, causes prices to rise in both our countries. And it's in our interests that we share technologies to move away from the era of fossil fuels....

So, Mr. Prime Minister, thank you very much for having me.

Prime Minister Singh: It's a great honor, Mr. President, to have you.

Question: Thank you, Mr. Prime Minister. Thank you, Mr. President. Sir, since you have said that India-U.S. nuclear cooperation agreement is on, what we would like to know from you is how are you going to ensure India's concerns and Indian scientific community's concerns regarding non-stop supply of fuel, and also protecting India's three-phased nuclear research program?

And excuse me, sir. Mr. President, I have a question for you too, sir. Sir, you know, everybody is saying that India and the

United States are natural allies. And you have also said many times that our strategic partnership is based on common values, shared values. Sir, then why the largest democracy of the world is reluctant or not forthcoming to support—the oldest democracy of the world is not supporting the largest democracy of the world to have a permanent membership of the United Nations Security Council? This is an issue India would like to hear from you more, sir. Thank you. Thank you, Prime Minister.

Prime Minister Singh: You have asked me about the nuclear agreement. As I mentioned, we have reached a mutually satisfactory understanding with regard to carrying forward the process that was outlined in the July 18 statement which I and President Bush signed.

An important step forward is the preparation of a separation plan, a separation plan which separates the civilian nuclear program from the military program. That phase has been successfully completed. Now it is for the United States to go to the Congress for necessary amendments in U.S. laws. Also, the U.S. will approach the members of the Nuclear Supplier Groups, and thereafter we'll also have to go to the International Atomic Energy Agency for India-specific safeguards.

So we have made very satisfactory progress. And I thank the President for his initiative. But for his leadership, this day would probably have not come so soon.

President Bush: Thank you for your question on the U.N. Security Council. I'm not surprised you asked it. As a matter of fact, I gave an interview to a person from the India media in Washington, D.C., prior to my trip, and that was one of the questions asked.

My answer hasn't changed, by the way, which is this. One, we support United Nations Security Council reform, and we're interested in different ways to reform the United Nations Security Council. My concern all along, however, is that if we only stick to the United Nations Security Council reform, we miss an opportunity to reform the United Nations overall. And so our position is, let's make sure reform overall moves forward, as we think about the best way to reform the Security Council.

The United Nations is a very important international body. It's one that does, however, require better accountability and — accountability on how we spend money and accountability on getting results. One such area, for example, is the Human Rights Commission. The Human Rights Commission needs to be reformed in a way that actually is able to achieve significant results on behalf of the world.

And so we're open-minded and we're listening. But what we don't want to do is have a Security Council reform measure that causes the other reforms not to go forward.

Suzanne, you probably need a microphone, unless you want to belt it out....

Question: President Bush, two questions for you. First—

President Bush: Only two? That's good.

Question: First, on the nuclear deal, how do you plan to sell the agreement to a very powerful non-proliferation lobby in Washington which has opposed the deal? And second, on the issue of terrorism, in the context of today's bomb blasts in Karachi, how do you propose to work with India on terrorism, considering India considers that the epicenter of terrorism is in Pakistan?

President Bush: Well, one way we work together on terrorism is to make sure intelligence services share information. The way you defeat terrorists is you—in the short-term—is you anticipate and react to their motives and their actions through good intelligence.

We're involved in a different kind of war. This is a war where people hide and plot and plan and then all of a sudden emerge and kill. And so it requires a different response. And part of the response is to commit our intelligence services to sharing information. We spent some time talking about that issue today.

As well, I will send—bring the same message to President Musharraf that we will continue to work with the President to share information to bring terrorists to justice. Terrorism is not prevalent only in this part of the world. It's prevalent in the

Middle East, as well. In the long run, terrorism will be defeated by giving people hope and opportunity, as opposed to systems of government which breed resentment and provide—and as a result of that resentment, provide opportunity for these killers to recruit.

In terms of convincing the Congress, the first thing I will say to our Congress is that our relationship is changing for the better. You know, sometimes it's hard to get rid of history, and short-term history shows that the United States and India were divided. We didn't have much of a relationship. And as a result, there are laws on the books that reflect that. Now the relationship is changing dramatically. People in the United States have got to understand that trade with India is in our interest, that diplomatic relations with India are in our interest, that cultural exchanges with India are in our interest.

One of the things that helps make that case, of course, is the —there's a lot of Indian Americans making important contributions to our country. And we welcome those contributions. I think there needs to be more student exchanges between our countries. I think we ought to expand H1B visas for Indian scientists and engineers and physicists and people in our country.

In other words, what I'm trying to explain to you is that it's a changing relationship, and part of that change is going to be how to deal with the nuclear issue. Now, proliferation is certainly a concern and a part of our discussions, and we've got a good faith gesture by the Indian Government that I'll be able to take to the Congress. But the other thing that our Congress has got to understand is that it's in our economic interests that India have a civilian nuclear power industry to help take the pressure off of the global demand for energy.

Obviously, nuclear power is a renewable source of energy, and the less demand there is for non-renewable sources of energy, like fossil fuels, the better off it is for the American people. Increasing demand for oil from America, from India and China, relative to a supply that's not keeping up with demand, causes our fuel prices to go up. And so, to the extent that we can reduce demand for fossil fuels, it will help the American consumer.

And so there are several ways for me to make the case, which I'm kind of laying out for you now, so that—but this is what I'll be telling our Congress.

Axelrod.

Question: Mr. President, Mr. Prime Minister, following up on this just a touch, what kind of message, sir, does it send to the world that India, which has been testing as late as 1998, nuclear testing, and is not—has not signed the Nuclear Non-Proliferation Treaty—is this a reward for bad behavior, as some critics suggest? And what kind of message does it send to other countries that are in the process of developing nuclear technology? Why should they sign the NPT if India is getting a deal without doing so, sir?

President Bush: What this agreement says is things change, times change, that leadership can make a difference, and telling the world—sending the world a different message from that which is—what used to exist in people's minds.

I—listen, I've always said this was going to be a difficult deal for the Prime Minister to sell to his parliament, but he showed great courage and leadership. And it's difficult for the American President to sell to our Congress, because some people just don't want to change and change with the times. I understand that. But this agreement is in our interest, and therefore, Jim, I'm confident we can sell this to our Congress as in the interest of the United States, and at the same time make it clear that there's a way forward for other nations to participate in a—in civilian nuclear power in such a way as to address non-proliferation concerns.

India has charted a way forward. You heard the Prime Minister talk about going to the IAEA. That group exists to help safeguard—safeguard the world from proliferation.

Listen, I proposed reprocessing agreements—that stands in stark contrast to current nuclear theology that we shouldn't reprocess for proliferation concerns. I don't see how you can advocate nuclear power, in order to take the pressure off our own economy, for example, without advocating technological development of reprocessing, because reprocessing will not only— reprocessing is going to help with the environmental concerns with nuclear power. It will make there—to put it bluntly, there will be less material to dispose.

And so I'm trying to think differently, not to stay stuck in the past, and recognize that by thinking differently, particularly on nuclear power, we can achieve some important objectives, one of which is less reliance on fossil fuels; second is to work with our partners to help both our economies grow; and thirdly is to be strong on dealing with the proliferation issues.

Well, Mr. Prime Minister, it's been a joy.

Prime Minister Singh: Thank you very much, Mr. President. We have made history today, and I thank you.

President Bush: Thank you, sir. Thank you.

U.S.-India Joint Statement

27

White House Press Release

Office of the Press Secretary

March 2, 2006

President George W. Bush and Prime Minister Manmohan Singh today expressed satisfaction with the great progress the United States and India have made in advancing our strategic partnership to meet the global challenges of the 21st century. Both our countries are linked by a deep commitment to freedom and democracy; a celebration of national diversity, human creativity and innovation; a quest to expand prosperity and economic opportunity worldwide; and a desire to increase mutual security against the common threats posed by intolerance, terrorism, and the spread of weapons of mass destruction. The successful transformation of the U.S.-India relationship will have a decisive and positive influence on the future international system as it evolves in this new century.

Reviewing the progress made in deepening the global partnership between the United States and India since their Joint Statement of July 18, 2005, the President and the Prime Minister reaffirm their commitment to expand even further the growing ties between their two countries. Consistent with this objective, the two leaders wish to highlight efforts the United States and India are making together in the following areas, where they have:

For Energy Security and a Clean Environment

(1) Welcomed the successful completion of discussions on India's separation plan and looked forward to the full implementation of the commitments in the July 18, 2005 Joint Statement on nuclear cooperation. This historic accomplishment will permit our countries to move forward towards our common objective of full civil nuclear energy cooperation between India

and the United States and between India and the international community as a whole.

(2) Welcomed the participation of India in the ITER initiative on fusion energy as an important further step towards the common goal of full nuclear energy cooperation.

(3) Agreed on India's participation in FutureGen, an international public-private partnership to develop new, commercially viable technology for a clean coal near-zero emission power project. India will contribute funding to the project and participate in the Government Steering Committee of this initiative.

(4) Welcomed the creation of the Asia Pacific Partnership on Clean Development and Climate, which will enable India and the U.S. to work together with other countries in the region to pursue sustainable development and meet increased energy needs while addressing concerns of energy security and climate change. The Partnership will collaborate to promote the development, diffusion, deployment and transfer of cleaner, cost-effective and more efficient technologies and practices.

(5) Welcomed India's interest in the Integrated Ocean Drilling Program, an international marine research endeavor that will contribute to long-term energy solutions such as gas hydrates.

(6) Noting the positive cooperation under the Indo-U.S. Energy Dialogue, highlighted plans to hold joint conferences on topics such as energy efficiency and natural gas, to conduct study missions on renewable energy, to establish a clearing house in India for coal-bed methane/coal-mine methane, and to exchange energy market information.

For Innovation and the Knowledge Economy

(1) Emphasizing the importance of knowledge partnerships, announced the establishment of a Bi-National Science and Technology Commission which the U.S. and India will co-fund. It will generate collaborative partnerships in science and technology and promote industrial research and development.

(2) Agreed that the United States and India would work together to promote innovation, creativity and technological

advancement by providing a vibrant intellectual property rights regime, and to cooperate in the field of intellectual property rights to include capacity building activities, human resource development and public awareness programs.

(3) Agreed to continue exploring further cooperation in civil space, including areas such as space exploration, satellite navigation, and earth science. The United States and India committed to move forward with agreements that will permit the launch of U.S. satellites and satellites containing U.S. components by Indian space launch vehicles, opening up new opportunities for commercial space cooperation between the two countries.

(4) Welcomed the inclusion of two U.S. instruments in the Indian lunar mission Chandrayaan-1. They noted that memoranda of understanding to be signed by ISRO and NASA would be significant steps forward in this area.

(5) Welcomed the U.S. Department of Commerce's plan to create a license exception for items that would otherwise require an export license to end-users in India engaged solely in civilian activities....

Briefing by Secretary Rice and National Security Advisor Hadley Aboard Air Force One

28

February 28, 2006

....Obviously, it starts with the cooperation in the war on terror. We have also—and that cooperation is good, it's continuing. One of the things that is part of this discussion over several years about enhancing U.S.-Indian civil nuclear cooperation, is that that is a vehicle for bringing India onto the same page as we are on the issue of proliferation. It is a way we can make India a global partner with this non-proliferation.

That also opens the door, of course, to cooperation with India on nuclear energy. And one of the things I think you will find coming out of this visit is that we are clearly moving in that direction with India. India is probably going to become and participate in the EDER initiative on nuclear fusion. They are going to participate in the FutureGen project. And we would hope, at some point, as we move forward under cooperation, that India would participate in the next generation nuclear program that the President has set out, GNEP (Global Nuclear Energy Partnership).

The cooperation with India in energy is also not just limited to the nuclear area. As you know, there is a regional Asian partnership with India, China, Japan, the United States and South Korea, in which we are working to develop energy initiatives that are providing energy security in the long-term, in a way that is environmentally responsible. These are just examples of United States and India cooperating together on solving global problems....

Question: So what is the status of the civil nuclear agreement? It doesn't sound like you're going to be able to get it done on this trip.

Secretary Rice: Well, we're still working on it, and we'd like to have a deal. Obviously, it's an important—would be an important breakthrough, not just for the United States and India, but also for the role of nuclear power in energy development, for our relationship with India on these global issues that Steve talked about. But as Steve said, I think when he briefed you on Friday, we'd very much like to have a deal; we're going to continue to work at it. But if we don't have one for this trip, then we will continue to work at it. It's very important.

The key here is that these are big and important issues. And the one thing that is absolutely necessary is that any agreement would assure that once India has decided to put reactors on safeguards, that it remains permanently under safeguards. So we've got a couple of issues that are important—and we'll keep talking about them—that remain unresolved. But we're going to keep working at it, whether or not there is a deal on this trip.

Question: Does the fast breeder reactor have to be under safeguards?

Secretary Rice: I think the key here is that India has to demonstrate that it is prepared to put its civilian reactors under safeguards, and do so permanently. There are a variety of ways that that might happen. I don't want to get too much into the discussions that we're having on particular types of reactors, but I think not every reactor and not every type is going to be under safeguards. I think that's what you're—

Question: Is that an exception then, for the fast breeder?

Secretary Rice: Terry, let's wait and see what the agreement says.

Question: Is there a concern that if an agreement isn't reached on this trip that momentum will be lost?

Secretary Rice: No, not at all. First of all, this trip is not a civil nuclear power trip. This trip is a trip about the relationship between the United States and India. It's business development, it's science and technology development, going back to agriculture. This is a very broad relationship that is deepening, and I think benefiting the world as it did, and cooperation on the tsunami, as it demonstrated in the IAEA Board of Governors, where India joined the consensus on Iran. So there's a lot that is going to be cemented here.

But the civil nuclear piece of it is important. And if they take some time to continue to work, we'll continue to work on it.

Mr. Hadley: But remember, the basic framework is something that was agreed last July, when the Prime Minister came to Washington. So we got the framework. The implementation is going to take a long period of time. The next stop in the implementation is this separation agreement, which is what we've been working on. But we've been working on this for four, five, six months; they come here, we go there; holding telephone conversations, exchanging documents. This is part of an implementation process of the basic agreement, which was reached last July.

So if you get it for the trip, that's fine. You always like to use trips as forming function or forcing functions. If we don't get it on the trip, then we'll get it after the trip, because the parties are committed to make this relationship work in the civil nuclear area.

Question: What do you say to those critics who say this agreement represents an end run around the Non-Proliferation Treaty?

Mr. Hadley: Just the opposite, as I said in my comments. This is actually a way to bring India within the non-proliferation framework. It will be adopting the kind of non-proliferation protections that we do. It's to bring India on the same page as we, so they can be a global partner, if you will, in the proliferation issue, as well. And India has had a good record, as a practical matter, in terms of proliferation to third countries. They've been a very responsible party. This is actually the vehicle to bring India onto our page, in terms of proliferation policy.

Secretary Rice: Let me just note that one of the supporters of the framework agreement has been Mohamed ElBaredei, of the IAEA, because he sees precisely what Steve just said, that this brings India into a framework that makes it a good partner on the proliferation side, which it has demonstrated that it can be over the years.

Question: Do you think that Pakistan qualifies for this same kind of special treatment?

Secretary Rice: Pakistan is not in the same place as India. I think everybody understands that. And one of the important contributions, or one of the important achievements I think of the administration is that we've been able to take Pakistan on its own terms and India on its own terms. We have programs and relationships with Pakistan that would not be appropriate with India, and vice versa. And I think that being able, in a sense, to de-link these two, and to have good relations with both, on their own terms, has both helped the relations—our relations with them, and I think it's helped their relations with each other.

Question: What about Afghanistan, do you want to say anything about whether or not we're going to go there?

Mr. Hadley: We're briefing India and Pakistan. That's the trip that we're talking to you about. And, obviously, if we have any changes to make in the schedule, we'll let you know in the normal course.

Question: Speaking of changes in the schedule, it seems like Friday night—there's a departure Friday night—

Mr. McClellan: Even if we were, we wouldn't be telling you until it was the appropriate time.

Question: Well, it's in the trip book. Can you say what we're doing Friday night?

Mr. Hadley: I will say this to you: If we make a change to the schedule, you'll be the first to know.

Question: I don't think so.

Question: Wait a minute, I want to know, too.

Mr. McClellan: All right, we're landing.

Press Briefing by National Security Advisor Steve Hadley on the President's Trip to India and Pakistan

29

Steve Hadley, National Security Advisor

February 24, 2006

Mr. Hadley: Good afternoon. Next week the President and Mrs. Bush will depart for South Asia. They will travel to India and Pakistan. This is the first trip of the President and Mrs. Bush to either country. They are very much looking forward to it.

In India, the President will participate in an arrival ceremony, and then a wreath-laying ceremony in honor of Mahatma Gandhi. The trip will basically celebrate a U.S.-Indian strategic partnership that is rooted in shared values and is broad in both its nature and scope.

The two countries are working together on a range of global issues, including counter-terrorism, non-proliferation, energy and the environment, and the expansion of economic and political freedom. The President will meet with Prime Minister Singh and the two will discuss the strong relationship between India and the United States and their cooperation on these global issues, and a variety of bilateral issues, as well....

And with that, I'll be glad to take your questions.

Question: Could you update us on Nick-Burns' negotiations in New Delhi? Are they over?

Mr. Hadley: As you know, the United States and India have been trying to negotiate a document pursuant to the joint statement reached last July of expanding civil nuclear cooperation between the United States and India. Pursuant to that, we have been trying for several weeks to negotiate an agreement whereby

India would separate its nuclear facilities between those that are for civil programs and those which are for military programs.

These negotiations have been ongoing for a while. Indians have come here, we have gone there. There have been exchange of papers, exchanges of phone calls. In this latest round, the Indians provided a document about a week ago; we provided some additional ideas and response. Nick Burns went to India. There have been good consultations. He is now coming back to Washington to report on where we are on those discussions. We're making progress, but we're not yet there. The Indians, hopefully, will have an opportunity from there end to see where we are. And we would expect those negotiations will continue by phone, document and the like, probably up through the President's—up to the President's visit.

We would, obviously, like, and the Indians would like to use the occasion of this visit to reach agreement on this so-called separation agreement. We think that would be a good thing. But it's important to have a good agreement that works for the Indians, works for the United States, will be acceptable to our Congress and to the nuclear suppliers group. And that's our objective. We'd like to get it before the trip. If we can, great. If we can't, we'll continue to negotiate it after the trip.

There's, as you could tell from the President's address, is a very broad and rich relationship between the United States and India right now, and the two leaders will have a lot to talk about, whether there's this agreement or not.

Question: Well, on that point, does the success or failure of the trip hinge on whether or not you get an agreement?

Mr. Hadley: Certainly not. As you could—listened from the President's speech, there is a long list of things that we are doing together with India, a long list of areas where we hope to have some things to announce during the trip that will demonstrate the breadth and intensity. So, look, it would be nice to have the separation agreement before the trip; if not, if we don't get it before the trip, we think we'll get it after the trip.

Question: What specifically is the hold up to a deal, Steve?

Mr. Hadley: It's just getting some clarification from the Indian side about what's in the civil side and what's on the military side, not only in terms of what exists now, at this time, but what are going to be the ground rules going forward. There are many of technical aspects to it. And the challenge, from the Indian side, of course, is this came up as an integrated program, and now they're having to make the kind of separation that we've made and other countries have made. And it's hard. It's an issue about facilities, about people, about organization. And it's just—it's taken time to work through. Again, we're trying to see if we can use the visit as a forcing function. If we can, great. If not, we'll continue to work on it after the visit is over.

Question: Is the President coming—taking with him anything else, let's say, if this nuclear agreement is not going to be—or any kind of agreement is going to be signed, either in India or Pakistan during this trip?

Mr. Hadley: Well, one of the things about this kind of relationship between India and the United States is that it's at the point where, in some sense, it's been institutionalized. When relations between two countries are in an early stage, everybody focuses on what's the deliverable for the trip, because in some sense, trips are the only times you get agreements and you move forward in the relationship.

A lot of the relationship is now institutionalized. There's a business dialogue, there's economic dialogue, there's energy dialogues, and a lot of those things have produced statements and agreements and joint programs that the President and the Prime Minister will be able to ratify and bless.

So I think there's going to be a lot of things. But, again, it's not three or four major initiatives. It's the kind of relationship whereby you'll see, I think, a range of agreements, understandings, next steps, across a broad range of issues that will show that the relationship is moving forward, and really is pretty institutionalized at this point....

Question: Steve, what would the President like to see from India on Iran during his visit, either in terms of the nuclear program there, or in terms of the Iran-Pakistan-India pipeline?

Mr. Hadley: I think India has, of course, been a participant in the IAEA Board of Governors. It has, in the two recent votes that were taken there, it has been in the side of those who really believe that Iran needs to be held to account for the non-compliance with the safeguards agreement, and that the issue needs to be referred to the U.N. Security Council. So I think it will be a reinforcement of that commitment.

I think what both leaders will do is step back and talk about more broadly the challenge that Iran poses for stability in the region. It is certainly an issue of Iran's effort to achieve nuclear weapons. It is also Iran's role as a state sponsor of terror; the support it is providing to countries like Syria, which are also involved in supporting terror; the attitude its government has towards Israel; the unconstructive role it's playing in terms of the Middle East; and the way it treats its own people.

The President, of course, on Wednesday and then again today, talked about the initiative that was announced by the Secretary of State to try and enhance our support for those voices within Iran that are calling for greater freedom and openness in that society. That's a very important thing in looking forward to the day when we have a democratic Iran that can be a partner on these issues, rather than to be a part of the problem on these issues.

So I think you'll find a kind of—a strategic level discussion between the two leaders on the challenge Iran poses and what we need to do about it together.

Question: Can you respond to the criticism that the nuclear deal rewards bad behavior and makes it harder for the United States to get help for the other countries that have operated outside the framework?

Mr. Hadley: I don't think it does. I think what the nuclear agreement does is it brings India into, and has India accepting the kinds of proliferation restrictions that the rest of the international community has accepted. Because the U.S-India civil nuclear is premised on India and the United States getting on the same page with respect to proliferation. The first step was the so-called NSSP—the next steps in strategic partnership—which we entered into over two years ago and which was completed in July. And as part of that, as the United States and India enhance their cooperation in the areas of space, high technology, civil nuclear, India was taking steps to bring its non-proliferation policies and practices in accord with ours and the international community, generally.

So I think, in fact, it is our view, and is the President's view, that the civil nuclear cooperation we contemplate with India will not only be good for India to help it deal with the enormous challenges it faces in its own development to find a clean, environmentally sound, and secure energy, but it also has the effect of bringing India on the same page as the rest of us in terms of the fight against nuclear proliferation....

Thank you very much.

Declaration by India and France on the Development of Nuclear Energy for Peaceful Purposes

30

February 20, 2006

India and France, recalling their deep ties of friendship and cooperation and the importance of the Strategic Dialogue established between them in January 1998, recognize that nuclear energy provides a safe, environmental friendly and sustainable source of energy. They underline the need to further develop international cooperation in promoting the use of nuclear energy for peaceful purposes. They believe that nuclear energy will provide an indispensable source of energy to future generations.

India and France consider that proliferation of nuclear, chemical and biological weapons, as well as their means of delivery constitute a threat to international peace and security. They share common concerns and objectives in the field of non-proliferation of weapons of mass destruction and their means of delivery including in view of possible linkages with terrorism.

India and France recall their past exchanges on civilian nuclear energy. They stress with satisfaction the development, since the creation of the Strategic Dialogue, of a fruitful bilateral dialogue on civil nuclear cooperation and on nuclear safety and, in accordance with their respective international obligations and commitments, the joint projects that are taking place as a result of this dialogue.

They recall that the joint statement issued by the President of the Republic of France and the Prime Minister of the Republic of India on 12 September 2005 stated that India and France would work towards the conclusion of a bilateral nuclear cooperation agreement. India and France affirm their willingness to further develop their cooperation in the use of nuclear energy exclusively for peaceful purposes under that agreement including in nuclear power generation, with a view to achieving sustainable development.

India and France recall the framework of the bilateral working group on energy established in January 1998, of the France-India Joint Committee for Atomic Energy created by the 16 September 2002 MoU signed between AEC (Atomic Energy Commission), India, and CEA (Commissariat a l'Energie Atomique), France, and of the dialogue between their Nuclear Safety Authorities launched by the 29 July 1999 Arrangement, renewed by the 24 October 2005 Arrangement between AERB (Atomic Energy Regulatory Board), India, and DGSNR (Direction Generale de la Surete Nucleaire et de la Radioprotection), France. They express their willingness to expand and strengthen their bilateral dialogue on peaceful uses of nuclear energy.

In accordance with the principles governing their respective nuclear policies, India and France confirm that they are engaging in discussions to conclude a bilateral cooperation agreement on the development of nuclear energy for peaceful purposes, subject to their respective international commitments and obligations. India and France look forward to adjustment of international civil nuclear cooperation framework with respect to India and confirm their intention to work to that end so that the agreement can be implemented fully.

In this respect, India and France share the same understanding of the following:

1. Cooperation under the future agreement may cover the following areas: basic and applied research not requiring the supply of uranium enriched to twenty (20) per cent or greater in the isotope U235; development and use of nuclear energy applications in the fields of agronomy, biology, earth sciences and medicine, and in industry; application of nuclear energy to power generation, including setting up of power projects; nuclear fuel management; nuclear waste management; nuclear safety, radioprotection and environmental protection; prevention of, and response to, emergency situations

resulting from radioactive or nuclear accidents; public awareness and acceptance of the benefits of the use of nuclear energy exclusively for peaceful purposes; and in any other field as jointly agreed by the Parties to that agreement.

2. Cooperation under the future agreement may take the following forms: exchange and training of scientific and technical staff; exchange of scientific and technical information; participation by scientific and technical staff of one Party in research and development activities conducted by the other Party; joint conduct of research and engineering activities, including joint research and experimentation (that is to say for which the two Parties are providing equivalent resources); organization of scientific and technical conferences and symposiums; provision of material, nuclear material, equipment, technology, facilities and services; consultations and cooperation in relevant international fora; and any other form of cooperation jointly agreed by the Parties to that agreement.
3. Agreements already signed between the concerned institutions of both countries such as DAE (Department of Atomic Energy) and CEA; BARC (Bhabha Atomic Research Centre) and IRSN (Institut de Radioprotection et de Surete Nucleaire); AERB and DGSNR in the field of atomic energy will become a part of this framework agreement and will continue to be implemented as at present.
4. India and France will ensure that cooperation pursuant to the future agreement shall be exclusively for peaceful purposes and covered where applicable by appropriate safeguards agreements with the IAEA. The cooperation agreement, and as appropriate, subsequent specific agreements, will also address issues relating to inter alia confidentiality of information, third party nuclear liability, intellectual property, measures relating to physical protection and retransfers to third States.

31

Remarks to the Press with Indian Foreign Secretary Shyam Saran and R. Nicholas Burns, Under Secretary for Political Affairs

January 20, 2006

Moderator: Good evening, ladies and gentlemen. Welcome to this joint press interaction between Foreign Secretary Mr. Shyam Saran and Under Secretary of State Mr. Nicholas Burns. This has to be a quick press interaction, so after the two opening remarks have been made, we have time only for a few questions because the Under Secretary has to catch a flight and the Foreign Secretary has another engagement at 5:00, so I will request the Foreign Secretary first to address the press.

Foreign Secretary Saran: Well, good evening to all of you. First of all, let me take this opportunity of welcoming Under Secretary Nicholas Burns. We have spent the last couple of days in very friendly and very intensive discussions on a whole range of issues. Let me begin by saying that a part of the discussions—a very important part of the discussions—was focused on the forthcoming landmark visit of President Bush and Mrs. Bush on a state visit to India, which we expect to take place sometime in the first week of March this year. I conveyed to Under Secretary Burns and his delegation that a very warm welcome awaits President Bush and Mrs. Bush to India. In our discussions, we looked at how this, the itinerary that we are looking at—both the protocol aspects as well as the substantive aspects of the visit—is really reflective of the very significant transformation that has taken place, and is taking place in India-U.S. relations. So we had a preliminary and a broad discussion on that agenda. And of course, it will be for the advance team that will be coming from Washington and further discussions that we have with our American friends to really get a fix on that itinerary for that very important visit. We both attach a great deal of importance to this visit. It would be really another defining moment in Indo-U.S. relations.

As you are aware we also had another meeting of the Joint Working Group on civil nuclear energy cooperation. As you know this group is headed by Under Secretary Burns on the U.S. side and myself on the Indian side. You would recall that when I had gone to Washington sometime back, I had shared with Under Secretary Burns some preliminary ideas about the kind of separation plan for our civil and military facilities that we were contemplating on the Indian side. We also discussed some other components of that proposed agreement, to which also we attach a lot of importance. For example we had a preliminary discussion about the kind of safeguards that we are looking at. We had a discussion about what is the kind of scope of our cooperation. A number of issues were discussed, but this was really the first time that we were going into some of the substantive aspects of the proposed agreement.

This current meeting that we had of the Joint Working Group enabled us to carry forward our discussions in much greater detail on all aspects of the proposed agreement. And it would be fair to say that, I think, we have today a much better understanding of the kind of perspectives that the United States has with regard to various aspects of this proposed agreement, and we have a much clearer perspective, as well. I think we have come to the conclusion that we need to discuss this in greater detail in the coming days and weeks. And this particular dialogue between us will be continued. In the course of these discussions, we have, for example, shared with the United States our plans for a very significant expansion of our civilian nuclear energy capability over the next few years, and what kind of scope of international cooperation that we envisage for meeting the targets that we have in the civil nuclear energy sector. So this has been an extremely useful discussion. It would be, as I said, fair to say that we need to have more discussions on this particular subject.

We also had occasion to exchange views on a number of regional issues. As you know, this aspect of our relationship has really developed in the recent past. We have been exchanging views and trying to coordinate our views on issues like Iran, on Nepal, Sri Lanka, and a number of these issues were discussed, although there was not so much time to go over the entire spectrum of regional issues. But we had a very useful discussion on some of these items. Under Secretary Burns will be visiting Pakistan, I believe, as well as Sri Lanka. So this was a good occasion for us to exchange notes, particularly since recently we have had the visit of President Rajapaksa to India. As you know, just a couple of days back I myself had a round of discussions with my Pakistani counterpart, so this was a very opportune moment for us to exchange notes on our relations with these countries.

So, once again this has been a very productive, very useful exchange of views—as always—and it has always been a pleasure to engage Nick in these very, very friendly, and very productive discussions. I look forward to having an opportunity to resume our dialogue in the none too distant future. Thank you very much, indeed.

Moderator: I now request Under Secretary Burns to address the press.

Under Secretary Burns: Thank you very much. Ladies and gentlemen, good afternoon. It is a pleasure to be here. I want to thank Foreign Secretary Shyam Saran for his hospitality to myself and to our delegation. We have had a very good two days of discussions here in Delhi. I was in Mumbai the day before that and I believe that President Bush is going to have a very interesting and very successful visit here when he comes later this year. We believe that the character and the quality of U.S.-Indian relations have been transformed by the last several years, particularly through the leadership of the Prime Minister and of our President. They have identified a strategic partnership on a global basis between India and the United States that is qualitatively different that any relationship that our two countries have, had going back to the founding and the independence of India in 1947. And so it is our strong, strong impression that across the board the foundations have been laid for a new relationship, both on the bilateral economic, and science and technology, and agriculture, and energy, and educational initiatives that the Prime Minister and President laid out in the July 18 statement. And of course to the cooperation on regional and global foreign policy issues that Foreign Secretary Saran outlined for you.

On that score, we do consider India to be a global partner. It is important that we talk about the situation in Sri Lanka. We are concerned about the situation there: concerned about the level of violence, concerned about the breakdown in the ceasefire. In my trip to Colombo in a couple of days, I will certainly be meeting with the Sri Lankan Government, meeting with my Norwegian colleagues as well, to try to make sure that we are standing on the side of the preservation of the cease fire and of peace and of a peaceful resolution of disputes there. In Nepal, the United States is very concerned by the actions of His Majesty the King in arresting and detaining members of the political establishment in the last couple of days, and we have issued a statement, frankly, very critical of that. We are equally critical, of course, of the Maoists. We believe that they should not be using violence as a political weapon. What India and the United States can do to get together to try to assert a joint appeal for peace and for democratic reconciliation in Nepal is very important.

And certainly, we had a very good discussion of Iran. You all know the position of my government. We believe that Iran is a threat to peace, both in its own region and globally. Iran has overstepped the bounds of international law in seeking to use its facility at Natanz for centrifuge research and enrichment. You have heard what our President and Secretary of State had to say about Iran during the last week. We had a thorough discussion of the situation with Foreign Secretary Saran.

We are hopeful that when the President visits, we will see a fruition of many of the joint initiatives that we have undertaken to strengthen the U.S.-India relationship. I mentioned some of them. I would say on the question of our future agreement on civil nuclear energy cooperation, we remain hopeful that we will be able to achieve this agreement. It is a very difficult undertaking, and it is a unique undertaking. I am not sure any two governments have actually had a negotiation quite like this, because the situation is unique, India's position is unique, and there is a complexity and a difficulty to these talks, which is inherent in the subject. Yet, we worked very well together for two days here. We listened to each other. I believe the American delegation learned a lot from what we heard from the Indian Government about its own perspective. Both Foreign Secretary Saran and I have committed to each other that we'll continue these talks, hopefully towards an agreement in the not too distant future.

So I am very pleased by the visit here. I think we have a great friend in India—we Americans. We are very grateful for the role that India is playing in the world today, and we are hopeful that this new relationship is going to go on to even greater heights in the future. I want to thank my good friend Foreign Secretary Shyam Saran for his hospitality and for his welcome that he has shown to myself and my delegation.

Moderator: First question this side, *New York Times*.

Question: (inaudible) Will Congress be inclined not to give India nuclear?

Foreign Secretary Saran: Well, as far as India is concerned, the civil nuclear energy cooperation agreement stands on its own merits, and whatever interaction we have had in the recent past with visiting Congressmen, visiting Senators, and the interaction that we have also had ourselves with Congressmen and Senators in Washington leads us to believe that there is a fund of goodwill for India in the U.S. Congress, that there is a very pervasive feeling of friendship and support—a bi-partisan support for a much stronger Indo-U.S. relationship. Therefore, we remain hopeful that the civilian nuclear energy cooperation Agreement, once it has been negotiated between the two Administrations, when it goes to the Congress, we remain hopeful that it will receive a positive response.

Moderator: Question at the back, *NDTV*.

Question: (inaudible) You describe the talks as being difficult and unique. From the papers submitted by India, do you feel that they are credible? And to Mr. Saran, do you agree with the EU and the U.S. on Iran?

Under Secretary Burns: Thank you very much. You know we set out in July—the Prime Minister and President set out—to undertake something new in international politics, and that is that the United States made a commitment to India, and India made some commitments to the United States, that we would try to overcome 30 years of division and disagreement on the civil-nuclear issue, that the United States would commit to make the argument to the Nuclear Suppliers Group as well as to the United States Congress that both U.S. law and international law and practice should be overturned to permit the international community to engage in trade, in technology transfer, in investment in India's civil nuclear energy. We think that proposition is an important one and will further the non-proliferation objectives of the international community, because the largest country in the world—the largest democracy in the world, India—will no longer be outside the system, but will be inside the system. And of course, that has enormous potential benefits for India. The benefits for the United States and the world community are that we'll be working with India—and engaging India—on an equal basis. And so they'll build benefits for both sides. It's a very attractive proposition.

What is unique and difficult, of course, is that this kind of thing has not been done before. India is a unique country, and its position on this particular issue and this industry is unique, obviously. And so, President Bush has taken the position that this is in the interests of the United States. It is in the interests of the other countries of the Nuclear Suppliers Group and we've had very good discussions in many different cities—in New York, in Washington, in Delhi, I think we have met in some European capitals, we have talked a lot on the phone—and I think what we've been able to do is establish a framework for how this agreement can work. We've now had a thorough discussion with the competent nuclear authorities of each government, by the way—in Foreign Secretary Saran's delegation, in my own delegation—about the intricacies and the details of this. And there's no question that we have made some progress over the last six months, but that much further progress has to be made, and that there are some difficulties ahead of us. But I have spent 25 years in diplomacy thinking that with goodwill and with dedication countries can reach agreements, and I have the same feeling about this agreement.

Question: (Inaudible).

Foreign Secretary Saran: We remain very supportive of the initiative taken by the European-3 to engage Iran in finding an amicable solution to some of the issues which have been raised with regard to the Iranian nuclear program. We have been extremely supportive of that process. And it stands to reason that, you know, India—which has with Iran a very long-standing, close, and what we call a 'civilizational' relationship with its people—that we would not like to see a situation of confrontation developing in a region that is very close to India. Therefore, our advice has always been that confrontation should be avoided. This is the message that we have given to our friends—this is a message which, by the way, we have also given to our Iranian friends—that an effort needs to be made in order to avoid a situation of confrontation from developing. We also believe that in dealing with this issue, it is important to develop as broad an international consensus as possible. And much of our effort over the last several weeks has been directed towards developing that international consensus. And that is the spirit in which we have also discussed this matter in the last couple of days, both with the United States of America, as also a representative of the EU-3, who has been on a visit to India recently, as well as with Iran.

Moderator: Thank you. *Associated Press.*

Question: (inaudible) You have been talking about difficulties in implementing this agreement. What are those difficulties?

Under Secretary Burns: I wish I had the luxury of taking you into the inside of these negotiations and telling you all the details, but I'm afraid that would violate all rules of diplomacy if I did that. Suffice it to say, I talked about the unique nature of these negotiations—given the history of the non-proliferation regime, given India's own history, in the nuclear sphere. I think that has added to the complexity of the negotiations, just by definition. There's no question that we believe—and we've said many times—that for any agreement to be credible with the United States Congress and the Nuclear Suppliers Group, it's going to have to be a detailed agreement, it's going to have to be substantial. Despite the fact that we've been at this for six months, I think there's still a further way to go. Both sides realize that, and we realize that we have our work cut out for us over the next several weeks. But we're dedicated, as a friend of India, to work on a respectful and equal basis with the Indian Government.

We'll have to see if we can be successful. I hope we can be I hope we can be, because it's very important that this agreement be realized. It's an agreement made between the President and the Prime Minister. It would have enormous benefits for India. It would really allow India to engage in international trade—in technology, in research and development—with other countries, with other scientific institutions, in a way that has not been possible for 30 years. It would allow the non-proliferation community, internationally—the regime that has been established internationally—to have the benefit of India meeting the same standards and practices in the civil sphere that all the rest of us have been meeting for a long time. We're negotiating on that basis, and we'll have to see what happens in the future. We'll be working hard, but there are difficulties ahead.

Question: A quick follow-up question: (inaudible) Are you going to be able to get this done before President Bush arrives?

Under Secretary Burns: I don't know for sure. Our goal, of course, would be to have an agreement before President Bush arrives in India. We would hope for that. Of course, nothing is ever certain in these types of negotiations, but what we have going for us is that there is a lot of trust between the Government of the United States and the Government of India. We feel that trust. We feel that we're negotiating with a highly professional set of diplomats on the Indian side; we know we have the goodwill of the Indian Government and they have ours. And in diplomacy that goes a long way. Both of us want to see the end of these negotiations, and want to see it move forward, and so we proceed on that basis.

Question: (inaudible) equating India's nuclear program with Iran and accusing the United States of double standards?

Under Secretary Burns: Well, I saw Dr. Larijani's remarks, which asserted this kind of double standard, and frankly, I think everyone was surprised by them. They were outrageous remarks from our perspective, because how is it possible to compare India with Iran in the nuclear sphere? On the one hand, you have a country—India—that has never been a proliferator, that has been very responsible in safeguarding its nuclear technology. On the other hand, you have a government and a regime in Iran, which the IAEA says for 18 years conducted secret nuclear research without revealing it to the IAEA; a government that just last week unilaterally lifted the seals placed by the IAEA on the centrifuge facility at Natanz—lifted it off unilaterally, said it would violate its agreement, in essence, with the European Union, by proceeding in nuclear research; a government that has earned the criticism of Russia, of China, of the European countries, of my own country, over the past two weeks.

I was in London earlier this week, meeting with the European-3 Governments, with the Russian and Chinese Governments, and while we don't have identical views on this—and I can't speak for those other governments—I can tell you what united us. Each of the governments that I mentioned that met in London this past Monday, just a couple of days ago, believes that Iran has crossed a line it should not have crossed. It should heed the advice of Dr. ElBaradei in the IAEA and return to negotiations. It should suspend its nuclear activities. It should not engage in centrifuge research, much less enrichment. My own government would say it should not engage in uranium conversion at the plant at Isfahan. So, Iran has clearly miscalculated. And the United States believes that there should be a vote of the IAEA Board of Governors on February 2nd, and there should be referral to the Security Council. Because, since Iran has crossed so many international red lines, Iran has to know that there's going to be a penalty to be paid for such actions. That's the American view on Iran. But for Dr. Larijani to assert somehow some equality between India and Iran by asserting a double standard is quite outrageous, and it's quite off the mark.

Moderator: Thank you very much.

Remarks to the Press at the American Center in Mumbai

32

R. Nicholas Burns, Under Secretary for Political Affairs

January 18, 2006

Question: On today's meetings in Mumbai, could you tell us something more about them? Did you meet, for instance, the Atomic Energy Commission Chairman? Did India's nuclear separation plan come up for discussion? Could you tell us what happened in these meetings today? Thank you.

Under Secretary Burns: Thank you very much. I'm primarily meeting members of the business community. I will not be meeting with the nuclear officials here. I will be meeting with atomic energy officials and also Foreign Secretary Saran in Delhi. But today I have met with a variety of people from the think tank community, the strategic community, from the business community. I'll be meeting Mr. Tata and his associates later this afternoon. Of course, he is the leader of the Indian part of the CEO Forum, which is a part of the initiative that Prime Minister Singh and President Bush initiated last July and which will be part of the future of this relationship.

So I'm just trying to get a sense—a better sense, a more refined sense—of what is possible in building a better economic relationship between us. There's a lot of work that can be done. Of course, most attention has been drawn to India-U.S. cooperation in the high-tech sector, and we've seen over the last two months major announcements by Microsoft and by Intel and by Cisco in the Indian high-tech sector. We've seen the announcement of the Boeing sale of civilian aircraft to the Indian authorities. And we obviously want to fill out that economic relationship, so today we have been talking about what we can do to increase U.S.-India cooperation in the agricultural sector, which is so important to India and my country. We had, in the 1950s, at the beginning of the U.S.-India relationship just after independence, a very full cooperation in agriculture. That has waned. Can we resuscitate that? And can we elevate our agricultural cooperation, say, between our universities, our land grant universities in the United States and the technical institutes that are so celebrated here in India? Can our two governments do more to see if we can work together in agricultural research?

Energy is the second field which is going to be very important for the future of the Indian economy and for our economy, and you've seen in recent weeks how important energy is on a global basis, looking at the Russia-Ukraine gas dispute, thinking through the problem of Iran, which is becoming a pariah country of sorts in the international community. So, energy is the second and infrastructure is the third. So, those are the issues we've been focusing on today and that I will continue to focus on in my discussions in Delhi.

Question: There are certain differences between the two countries about civilian nuclear cooperation? Have these differences been ironed out now? These negotiations have taken a lot of time. What are the outstanding issues? Where is the problem coming from? What are your apprehensions regarding this?

Under Secretary Burns: I wouldn't say there's any problem whatsoever, but this is very challenging, and what we have embarked upon, India and the United States, is an absolutely unique venture in international diplomacy. The United States has committed, along with India, to try to achieve a civil-nuclear agreement between the two countries. That will entail talking about issues that we haven't talked about for the last 30 years. We're now bringing them to the surface, and we are trying to implement the July 18 agreement as faithfully as we can, in a way that will benefit both countries. So there's no problem that is insuperable, but we have embarked on a unique diplomatic venture that does require, I think, the full six or eight months that it going to take to decide on how best to proceed, to put that into a bilateral agreement that President Bush and Prime

Minister Singh can then agree upon finally as the way ahead. And I have—of course, there are a number of differences as you go along; there are a number of complications—but I have confidence that we will reach this agreement and I think that there has been consensus on both sides, as well.

Question: What about the differences over the separation between India's civilian and military nuclear energy facilities? (Inaudible...) Have you sorted them out, and can we expect some announcement during President George W. Bush's India visit in March?

Under Secretary Burns: Well, if you look back at the July 18 statement that was issued at the White House, the joint statement, it does talk about India achieving a separation between its civilian and military nuclear facilities. And that is an enormously complex task. And that is at the heart of these negotiations, and I will be getting into details of that with my friend Foreign Secretary Saran tomorrow morning.

Question: The U.S. has expressed apprehensions over the Iran-India gas pipeline through Pakistan, following which there has been a re-think on the Indian side. Do you see any problems in this now?

Under Secretary Burns: Well, I think we had discussions, obviously, from time to time about this issue in diplomatic circles. I think...I know Secretary Rice has commented upon this in the past. I will obviously support what she said on this. And I think that it is an issue that is—the issue of Iran in general has become a major issue in global politics just over the last several months.

All of us need to think about our relations with Iran. Here is a country that, since August, has a radical government in place; a government that very recently has called for the destruction of a member-state of the United Nations, Israel; that has denied the historical basis of a holocaust that occurred during Second World War; a country that insists on its rights to enrich and reprocess uranium but doesn't talk much about its obligations and responsibilities in the international system. And I would just refer you to the remarks made by Dr. ElBaradei in his *Newsweek* interview published on Monday and the statement issued by the Russian foreign ministry last week, as well as the statements issued by my government and the European governments.

There is a great deal of frustration in the international community right now, and I think that there is a consensus that Iran should turn back, should return to negotiations, suspend its nuclear activities and discuss this issue in a rational and productive way. And that is not the course that Iran is on right now. And thus the great concern in my government and in my country and around the world about Iran.

Question: I have two questions, one related to Iran only. Unfortunately, if Iran does not come to the negotiating table, then what will be the options left for the U.S. and the world? And secondly, have you identified the civilian and military nuclear structures of India?

Under Secretary Burns: On the first question, Secretary Rice said the other day that we haven't left diplomacy behind, we've simply entered a different phase of diplomacy. There was an attempt made over the last two years, by the European Union governments, to negotiate with Iran in a peaceful and productive way, and the Iranians walked away from those negotiations unilaterally. And then last week they unilaterally took the seals off their nuclear plant at Natanz and said they would engage in centrifuge research, which we think is a quite dangerous step. So now we are suggesting a new phase in the diplomacy, and we are dedicated to a diplomatic solution to this problem—and that is to have the International Atomic Energy Agency refer the issue of Iran to the Security Council, because the Security Council is the supreme international multilateral body. It is the place where questions like this should be discussed, and a bright spotlight should be put upon the Iranian regime. And the Iranian regime should answer questions that all the world has about its nuclear intentions. And so, this is the next phase of diplomacy that we are embarking on, and as I said before we are very strong support for the European-3 in their quest to see these negotiations resumed.

On your second question: I really don't want to get into the details of the discussions that I'll have with the Foreign Secretary Saran, because I think that they're best left to the diplomatic...left to the privacy of the diplomatic conference table in the next couple of days, except to say that these are serious issues and they've got to be addressed seriously by both of our governments. I think they are, and we hope very much for a successful conclusion.

I should also say that, in addition to discussing the civil-nuclear issues, Prime Minister Singh and President Bush agreed upon a number of, in essence, joint ventures between the two governments in July. We now need to advance in those joint ventures: in agriculture; in higher education; in space launch; in welcoming an Indian astronaut into the American space program for the shuttle missions; in energy; in business promotion; in education. We have 80,000 Indian students in the United States, the greatest number of foreign students of any country. And so there's a lot that we can build on, and all of these initiatives are important. So I'll be discussing all those issues with the Foreign Secretary and his delegation.

And finally, we find India to be a very effective and very reliable partner in trying to work together to promote stability in South Asia. Both of us are concerned by the situation in Nepal. Neither of us wants to see a return to violence in Nepal by the Maoists. Both of us want to see the King, His Majesty the King, return to a democratic foundation. In Sri Lanka, I think it's fair to say we want to see a strengthening of the cease-fire agreement, an end to the violence that we've seen over recent weeks, in the attacks in recent weeks. In Bangladesh, we'd like to see the government respond vigorously to the challenge of violence and of religious extremism that have been all too evident in Bangladesh over the last several months. In Afghanistan, we wish to support President Karzai, and we will both be attending, India and the United States, a major international conference in London on January 31 to support the Afghan people and to pledge additional economic assistance and support for the government. And, of course, the United States wishes for the best relationship between Pakistan and

India. And so, we will be discussing all of these issues in Delhi over the next couple of days because they are a big, growing and, I think, increasingly important part of this relationship.

Thank you very much. Thank you for your attention and thank you for the questions you have asked. It's been a pleasure.

Hearing on U.S.-India Civil Nuclear Cooperation Initiative

33

Robert G. Joseph, Under Secretary for Arms Control and International Security

November 2, 2005

Chairman Lugar, Senator Biden, distinguished members of the Committee, it is an honor to appear before you today to discuss the President's policy toward India with respect to civil nuclear cooperation. I look forward to working with you over the months ahead to bring this important objective to a timely and successful outcome.

Toward U.S.-India Civil Nuclear Cooperation

We believe it is in our national security interest to establish a broad strategic partnership with India that encourages India's emergence as a positive force on the world scene. Our desire to transform relations with India is founded upon a contemporary and forward-looking strategic vision. India is a rising global power and an important democratic partner for the United States. Today, for the first time, the United States and India are bound together by a strong congruence of interests and values. We seek to work with India to win the global War on Terrorism, to prevent the spread of weapons of mass destruction and the missiles that could deliver them, to enhance peace and stability in Asia, and to advance the spread of democracy. India and the United States are on the same side of these critical strategic objectives. Our challenge is to translate our converging interests into shared goals and compatible strategies designed to achieve these aims.

In the context of this growing partnership, the United States and India reached a landmark agreement in July to work toward full civil nuclear cooperation while at the same time strengthening the nuclear non-proliferation regime. The Joint Statement agreed to by President Bush and Prime Minister Singh is not—as some have argued—a triumph of power politics over non-proliferation principles. This is not a zero-sum trade-off, whereby improvement in our bilateral strategic relationship results in non-proliferation losses. Rather, as the broadly-constituted Joint Statement is implemented, it will prove a win for our strategic relations, a win for energy security, and a win for non-proliferation.

India believes, and our Administration agrees, that it needs nuclear power to sustain dynamic economic growth and to address its growing energy requirements in an affordable and environmentally-responsible manner. Our goal—in the context of the Joint Statement—is to provide India access to the technology it needs to build a safe, modern and efficient infrastructure that will provide clean, peaceful nuclear energy.

At the same time, India has clearly demonstrated over the past several years its desire to work with the United States and the international community to fight the spread of sensitive nuclear technologies. As part of an effort launched with India during the Administration's first term—the Next Steps in Strategic Partnership—India took a number of significant steps to strengthen export controls and to ensure that Indian companies would not be a source of future proliferation. Not only did India pledge to bring its export control laws, regulations, and enforcement practices in line with modern export control standards, but also passed an extensive export control law and issued an upgraded national control list that will help it achieve this goal. In addition, India has become a party to the Convention on the Physical Protection of Nuclear Material and has taken significant steps toward meeting its obligations under UNSCR 1540.

The additional non-proliferation commitments India made as part of the Joint Statement go even further and, once implemented, will bring it into closer conformity with international nuclear non-proliferation standards and practices. This is a very important move for India and for the non-proliferation community. While we will continue to work with India and to encourage it to do more over time, India's implementation of its commitments will, on balance, enhance our global non-proliferation efforts. We expect the international nuclear non-proliferation regime will emerge stronger as a result.

As evidence of this expectation, we note with satisfaction India's positive IAEA Board of Governors vote in September on Iranian non-compliance, and look forward to further cooperative action on this critical international security issue.

Non-proliferation Gains

Through the Joint Statement, India has publicly committed to a number of important non-proliferation steps. It will now:

- Identify and separate civilian and military nuclear facilities and programs and file a declaration with the International Atomic Energy Agency (IAEA) regarding its civilian facilities;
- Place voluntarily its civilian nuclear facilities under IAEA safeguards;
- Sign and adhere to an Additional Protocol with respect to civilian nuclear facilities;
- Continue its unilateral moratorium on nuclear testing;
- Work with the U.S. for the conclusion of a multilateral Fissile Material Cut-Off Treaty (FMCT) to halt production of fissile material for nuclear weapons;
- Refrain from the transfer of enrichment and reprocessing technologies to states that do not have them and support efforts to limit their spread; and
- Secure nuclear and missile materials and technologies through comprehensive export control legislation and adherence to the Missile Technology Control Regime (MTCR) and Nuclear Suppliers Group (NSG).

India's commitment to separate its civil and military facilities and place its civil facilities and activities under IAEA safeguards demonstrates its willingness to assume full responsibility for preventing proliferation from its civil nuclear program. It will also help protect against diversion of nuclear material and technologies to India's weapons program.

By adopting an Additional Protocol with the IAEA, India will commit to reporting to the IAEA on exports of all NSG

Trigger List items. This will help the IAEA track potential proliferation elsewhere, and bolster our efforts to encourage all states to adopt an Additional Protocol as a condition of supply.

By committing to adopt strong and effective export controls, including adherence to NSG and MTCR Guidelines, India will help ensure that its companies do not transfer sensitive weapons of mass destruction and missile-related technologies to countries of concern. In July, India took an important step by harmonizing its national control list with the NSG Guidelines and by adding many items that appear on the MTCR Annex.

India has also committed to work with the United States toward the conclusion of a multilateral FMCT, which, if successfully negotiated and ratified, will ban the production of fissile material for use in nuclear weapons or other nuclear explosive devices.

India's pledge to maintain its nuclear testing moratorium contributes to non-proliferation efforts by making its ending of nuclear explosive tests one of the conditions of full civil nuclear cooperation. Since to date Pakistan has test-exploded nuclear weapons only in response to Indian nuclear tests, this commitment will help diminish the prospects for future nuclear testing in South Asia.

By committing not to export enrichment and reprocessing technology to states that do not already have such fully-functioning capabilities, India will help us achieve the goals laid out by President Bush in February 2004, designed to prevent the further spread of such proliferation sensitive equipment and technology. This will help close what is widely recognized as the most significant loophole in the Nuclear Non-proliferation Treaty regime—a loophole that has clearly been exploited by countries such as North Korea and Iran and could be manipulated by others in the future.

Each of these activities is significant. Together, they constitute a substantial shift in moving India into closer conformity with international non-proliferation standards and practices. Their successful implementation will help to strengthen the global non-proliferation regime.

As befits a major, responsible nation, and in keeping with its commitment to play a leading role in international efforts to prevent WMD proliferation, we hope that India will also take additional non-proliferation-related actions beyond those specifically outlined in the Joint Statement. We view this as a key component of the developing U.S.-India strategic partnership and look forward to working with the Indian Government, as well as the international community more broadly, to further strengthen non-proliferation efforts globally.

Through our ongoing bilateral dialogue we have already discussed with India such steps as endorsing the Proliferation Security Initiative Statement of Principles, bringing an early end to the production of fissile material for weapons, and harmonizing its control lists with those of the Australia Group and the Wassenaar Arrangement.

U.S. Commitments Under the Joint Statement

On a reciprocal basis with India's commitments, the United States has committed to work to achieve full civil nuclear cooperation with India. In this context, President Bush told Prime Minister Singh that he would:

- Seek agreement from Congress to adjust U.S. laws and policies;
- Work with friends and allies to adjust international regimes to enable full civil nuclear energy cooperation and trade with India; and
- Consult with partners on India's participation in the fusion energy International Thermonuclear Experimental Reactor (ITER) consortium and the Generation IV International Forum, the work of which relates to advanced nuclear energy systems.

To implement effectively the steps under the Joint Statement, we will need the active support of Congress and that of our international partners. We expect—and have told the Indian Government—that India's follow-through on its commitments is essential to success. We believe that the Government of India understands this completely and we expect them to begin taking concrete steps in the weeks ahead.

International Responses to Date

Mr. Chairman, since the July statement, we have actively engaged with our international partners—both bilaterally and in such multilateral fora as the G-8 and the Nuclear Suppliers Group. I have met directly with my counterparts from many different countries. Secretary Rice and other senior U.S. officials discussed the initiative with states at the recent UN General Assembly and at IAEA General Conference meetings. Assistant Secretaries Stephen Rademaker and Christina Rocca both travelled to Vienna to make presentations to the NSG Consultative Group. And, of course, many of our embassies have been actively engaged on this front.

While some countries, such as Sweden, have expressed substantial doubts about the initiative for fear of inadvertent damage to the nuclear non-proliferation regime, others have expressed strong support. For example, the UK has "warmly welcome(d)" this initiative and indicated that on the basis of the Joint Statement it was "ready to discuss with our international partners the basis for cooperation in civil nuclear matters with India". Similarly, France has underscored the "need for full international civilian nuclear cooperation with India". The Director General of the IAEA has also welcomed India's decision to place its civil nuclear facilities under safeguards and to sign and implement the Additional Protocol as "concrete and practical steps toward the universal application of IAEA safeguards".

To date, many other countries have adopted a "wait-and-see" approach. Most recognize the need to come to terms with India and not to allow it to remain completely outside the international non-proliferation system. They welcome the non-proliferation steps India has committed to take in the context of the Joint Statement. At the same time, they have made clear that their ultimate support will depend on the scope and pace of India's actions.

Some have understandably questioned how this complex initiative comports with the NPT and our efforts to combat WMD proliferation. Others have asked whether the provision of civil nuclear technology to India would be consistent with their obligations under the NPT not to contribute to India's nuclear weapons program. Still others have asked why a cap on India's production of fissile material for weapons was not part of the deal.

We have sought to clarify that the United States does not and will not support India's nuclear weapons program. As it is for other states, this is a "red line" for us. We are obligated under the NPT not to assist India's nuclear weapons program. Our initiative with India does not recognize India as a nuclear weapon State, and we will not seek to renegotiate the NPT, whether to change the Treaty definition of a nuclear weapon State or in any other way. We remain cognizant of, and will fully uphold, all of our obligations under the Nuclear Non-proliferation Treaty, and we remain committed in principle to universal NPT adherence.

But we also recognize that India is in a unique situation and has shown to be responsible in not proliferating its nuclear technologies and materials. With its decision to take the steps announced in the Joint Statement, India will now take on new non-proliferation responsibilities that will strengthen global non-proliferation efforts that serve the fundamental purpose of the NPT.

India has informed us that it has no intention of relinquishing its nuclear weapons or of becoming a party to the NPT as a non-nuclear weapon State, the only way it could adhere under the current terms of the Treaty. Despite this, it is important to seize this opportunity to assist India in becoming a more constructive partner in our global non-proliferation efforts. Indian commitments to be undertaken in the context of the Joint Statement will align Delhi more closely with the nuclear non-proliferation regime than at any time previously. India has said it wants to be a partner and is willing to take important steps to this end. We should encourage such steps.

In this context, it is important to note that the NPT does not ban civil nuclear cooperation with safeguarded facilities in India, nor does it require full scope safeguards as a condition of supply. In fact, under the "grandfather" provision of the NSG Guidelines, Russia today is building two nuclear reactors in India.

The NPT does preclude any cooperation that would "in any way assist" India's nuclear weapons program. For that reason, we have made clear that, under our proposal, supplier states will only be able to engage in cooperation with safeguarded facilities. Moreover, the more civil facilities India places under safeguards, the more confident we can be that any cooperative arrangements will not further any military purposes. We expect—and have indicated to the Government of India—that India's separation of its civil and military nuclear infrastructure must be conducted in a credible and transparent manner, and be defensible from a non-proliferation standpoint. In other words, the separation and the resultant safeguards must contribute to our non-proliferation goals. Many of our international partners have similarly indicated that they view this as a necessary precondition, and will not be able to support civil nuclear cooperation with India otherwise. We believe that the Indian government understands this.

With respect to the cessation of fissile material production, we continue to encourage India, as well as Pakistan, to move in this direction as part of our strategic dialogues with both governments. But we think it would be unwise to hold up the non-proliferation gains that can be obtained from the civil nuclear cooperation initiative for an Indian fissile material cap. Moreover, in the context of the Joint Statement, we jointly committed to work toward the completion of an effective Fissile Material Cut-Off Treaty. As we have indicated previously, the United States also stands willing to explore other intermediate options that also might serve this objective.

As India completes the significant actions that it has committed to undertake in the Joint Statement, we are convinced that the non-proliferation regime will emerge stronger. Separately, we will continue to encourage additional steps, such as India's acceptance of a fissile material production moratorium or cap, but we will not insist on it for the purposes of the civil nuclear cooperation initiative announced by the President and Prime

Minister. Even absent such a cap, the initiative represents a net gain for non-proliferation.

Key Challenges

Five key challenges face the successful achievement of Joint Statement implementation. These are: developing a meaningful civil/military separation; negotiating the appropriate safeguards arrangement; building support within the NSG; avoiding the temptation to renegotiate the deal; and securing domestic legal reform.

Developing a meaningful civil/military separation: We have indicated that the separation of civil and military facilities must be both credible and transparent, as well as defensible from a non-proliferation standpoint. We have engaged in initial discussions with the Government of India, and look forward to further discussion of a mutually acceptable approach. While India has not yet presented a formal separation plan, we are encouraged by Foreign Secretary Saran's public acknowledgements both that "it is legitimate for our partners to expect that such cooperation will not provide any advantage to our strategic programme", and that "it makes no sense for India to deliberately keep some of its civilian facilities out of its declaration for safeguards purposes, if it really is interested in obtaining international cooperation on as wide a scale as possible".

In our discussions to date, and in particular during Under Secretary Burns' recent talks in Delhi, we have discussed some straightforward principles. I will not enumerate them fully here since the negotiations remain ongoing, but would like to underscore just a couple of these. For example, to ensure that the United States and other potential suppliers can confidently supply to India and meet our obligations under the NPT, safeguards must be applied in perpetuity. Further, the separation plan must ensure—and the safeguards must confirm—that cooperation does not "in any way assist" in the development or production of nuclear weapons. In this context, nuclear materials in the civil sector should not be transferred out of the civil sector.

Negotiating the appropriate safeguards arrangement: India's voluntary commitment to allow IAEA safeguards on its civil facilities is both a substantial non-proliferation gain and a key enabler for nuclear energy cooperation. A critical bellwether of Indian intentions will be how it handles the separation and safeguarding of its civil nuclear infrastructure. In our discussions with key international partners, both in the NSG context and otherwise, many have expressed strong views that India's separation plan be transparent and have noted the importance of IAEA safeguards being applied to its civil facilities.

In this context, several countries have argued that it is integral to maintaining the integrity of the global regime that India not be granted *de jure* or *de facto* status as a nuclear weapon State under the NPT. For this reason, many have indicated that a "voluntary offer" arrangement of the type in place in the five internationally-recognized nuclear weapon States would not be acceptable for India. We indicated at the recent G-8 and NSG meetings that we would not view a voluntary offer arrangement as defensible from a non-proliferation standpoint or consistent with the Joint Statement, and therefore do not believe that it would constitute an acceptable safeguards arrangement. Such a course of action would in all likelihood preclude NSG support. Conversely, should India put forward a credible and defensible plan, we anticipate that many states will become more steadfast in their support.

Building support within the NSG: At the recent NSG Consultative Group meeting in Vienna, the United States discussed the initiative with regime members. We stressed our desire that the NSG maintain its effectiveness, and emphasized that we do not intend to undercut this important non-proliferation policy tool. For this reason, the U.S. proposal neither seeks to alter the decision-making procedures of the NSG nor amend the current full-scope safeguards requirement in the NSG Guidelines. Rather, the United States proposes that the NSG take a policy decision to treat India as an exceptional case, given its energy needs, its nuclear non-proliferation record, and the non-proliferation commitments it has now undertaken. We do not advocate similar treatment for others outside the NPT regime.

In our view, once India makes demonstrable progress in implementing key Joint Statement commitments—with a credible, transparent, and defensible separation plan foremost on the list—we will be ready to engage with our NSG partners in developing a formal proposal to allow the shipment of Trigger List items and related technology to India. Obviously, the number of facilities and activities that India places under IAEA safeguards, and the method and speed with which it does so, will directly affect the degree to which we will be able to build support for full civil nuclear cooperation. We look forward to discussing this more fully with NSG members at the Consultative Group meeting in early 2006 and at the plenary session that follows.

Avoiding the temptation to renegotiate the deal: Some observers—both in the United States and abroad—have argued that the U.S.-India arrangement as negotiated by the President and the Prime Minister does not constitute a net gain for non-proliferation, or at least does not reflect the maximum gain we might in theory have achieved. According to this view, the United States, presumably the U.S. Congress, should condition U.S. nuclear cooperation under the Joint Statement on additional Indian steps, such as implementing a moratorium on fissile material production, ratifying the Comprehensive Test Ban Treaty, and/or joining the NPT as a non-nuclear weapon state. Based on our interactions with the Indian government, we believe that such additional conditions would likely be deal-breakers.

This is a case where the "perfect" is the enemy of the "good", and we must resist the temptation to pile-on conditions that will prejudice our ability to realize the important and long-standing non-proliferation objectives embodied in the Joint Statement. We are better off with India undertaking the commitments it has now agreed to rather than allowing the *status quo* to prevail.

The Joint Statement reached by President Bush and Prime Minister Singh is good both for India and for the United States, and offers a net gain for global non-proliferation efforts. Rather than layer on additional conditions or seek to renegotiate the Joint Statement, it would be better to lock-in this deal and then seek to achieve further results in subsequent non-proliferation discussions. We believe that this is a sound arrangement that should be supported because the commitments India has made will, when implemented, bring it into closer alignment with international nuclear non-proliferation standards and practices and, as such, strengthen the global non-proliferation regime.

Securing domestic legal reform: The President promised in the Joint Statement that the Administration would seek agreement from Congress to adjust U.S. laws and policies. We recognize that the pace and scope of civil nuclear cooperation requires close consultations between the Executive and Legislative Branches. In our own ongoing review, we have identified a number of options for modifying and/or waiving provisions of the Atomic Energy Act that currently prohibit the United States from engaging in such cooperation with India.

As Under Secretary Burns noted, we do not intend to ask Congress to take legislative action until the Indian government takes certain important steps. We welcome your partnership as we embark on this effort, and look forward to working with your Committee, together with your House counterparts, as we jointly consider the best way forward in the legislative area.

Bottom Line: Advancing Non-proliferation

We must recognize that there is today no viable cookie-cutter approach to non-proliferation; we need tailored approaches that solve real-world problems. We need to be creative and adjust our approaches to take into account the conditions that exist, so that we can achieve our non-proliferation objectives. This has been a premise of Administration policy since the outset of President Bush's first term, in which he established non- and counter-proliferation as top national security priorities. He put in place the first comprehensive strategy at the national level for combating this pre-eminent threat to our security, and he embarked on changing how we as a nation, and how the international community more broadly, design and expand our collective efforts to defeat this complex and dangerous challenge.

Indeed, recognizing that traditional non-proliferation measures were essential but no longer sufficient, the President has established new concepts and new capabilities for countering WMD proliferation by hostile states and terrorists.

- He sought increased national resources to prevent proliferation through Nunn-Lugar type non-proliferation assistance programs and, through the G-8 Global Partnership, successfully enlarged the contributions from other countries to this essential task.
- He launched the Proliferation Security Initiative to disrupt the trade in proliferation-related materials. This initiative has achieved the support of more than seventy other countries who are working together to share information and develop operational capabilities to interdict shipments at sea, in the air, and on land.
- He initiated the effort resulting in the unanimous adoption of UN Security Council Resolution 1540, which requires all states to enact both legislation criminalizing proliferation activities under their jurisdiction and effective export controls to help protect the sensitive materials and technologies on their territories.

These efforts in effective multilateralism, coupled with the strengthening of our own counter-proliferation capabilities, have produced concrete successes such as the unraveling of the A.Q. Khan network and the decision by Libya to abandon its nuclear, chemical and long-range missile programs.

Similarly, we must pursue approaches with respect to India that recognize the reality that it is a growing 21st century power, shares our democratic values, has substantial and growing energy needs, and has long possessed nuclear weapons outside the NPT. *Status quo* approaches have not acknowledged these pragmatic considerations, nor have they achieved the positive outcome of progressively integrating India into the international nuclear non-proliferation mainstream.

We have begun consultations with our international partners; have conducted a number of introductory discussions with you, your colleagues, and your staff; and look forward to working further with you on the steps necessary to realize the benefits of the July Joint Statement.

U.S.-India Civilian Nuclear Cooperation

34

July 22, 2005

The United States has established a global partnership with India which encourages India's emergence as a positive force on the world scene. The U.S. and India have agreed that India should receive the benefits and accept all the responsibilities of the world's leading states with advanced nuclear technology, concurrent with its enhanced non-proliferation commitments and in the context of its growing energy needs. The agreement to reach full civil nuclear cooperation brings India into the international non-proliferation mainstream. It opens new doorways for a cleaner and more secure global energy future. It makes the United States an essential partner as India normalizes its rising position in the community of nations.

India will assume the same responsibilities and practices as other countries with advanced nuclear programs, and has agreed to:

- Identify and separate civilian and military nuclear facilities and programs and file an IAEA declaration regarding its civilian facilities;
- Place voluntarily its civilian nuclear facilities under IAEA safeguards;
- Sign and adhere to an Additional Protocol with respect to civilian nuclear facilities;
- Continue its unilateral moratorium on nuclear testing;
- Work with the U.S. for the conclusion of a multilateral Fissile Material Cut-off Treaty;

- Refrain from the transfer of enrichment and reprocessing technologies to states that do not have them and support efforts to limit their spread; and
- Secure nuclear materials and technology through comprehensive export control legislation and adherence to the Missile Technology Control Regime and Nuclear Suppliers Group.

The United States has reciprocally promised that the Administration will:

- Seek agreement from Congress to adjust U.S. laws and policies;
- Work with friends and allies to adjust international regimes to enable full civil nuclear energy cooperation and trade with India; and
- Consult with partners on India's participation in the fusion energy consortium—ITER and support India's part in work to develop advanced nuclear reactors.

Indian commitments to uphold central non-proliferation norms pave the way forward for expanded cooperation in the civil nuclear sphere. The agreement strengthens energy security and promotes the development of stable and efficient energy markets in India to ensure adequate, affordable energy supplies. These actions firmly align the U.S. with the world's largest democracy.

Epilogue

June 28: House International Affairs Committee of the United States cleared the bill relating to Indo-U.S. nuclear deal 37–5.

June 29: Senate Foreign Affairs Committee cleared the bill 16–2.

July 26 : America's House of Representatives cleared the landmark Indo-U.S. nuclear deal 359–68 (Legislation H.R. 5682, India-U.S. Nuclear Cooperation Promotion Act of 2006):

Votes in Favor:	Republicans	218
	Democrats	141
	Total	359
Votes Against:	Republicans	9
	Democrats	59
	Total	68

Decisions on Killer Amendments in the House of Representatives:

(i) U.S. to annually audit India's fissile material:
Defeated 155–268

(ii) Export of uranium to India restricted until the U.S. President certifies that India has frozen fissile material production:
Defeated 184–241

(iii) Deal to be linked to Indian support to U.S. against Iran:
Defeated 192–235

(iv) Nuclear cooperation only for peaceful productive purposes and not military:

Cleared 414–0

The Course Ahead:

(i) The American Senate will take up Bill S. 3709 later in 2006 for voting.

(ii) The Bush administration will have to win the support of the 45 member Nuclear Suppliers Group.

(iii) India will have to negotiate a separate pact with the International Atomic Energy Agency.